THE ROLLING STONES

The Story of the Band Series

Green Day: A Musical Biography
Kjersti Egerdahl

U2: A Musical Biography
David Kootnikoff

The Beatles: A Musical Biography
Kate Siobhan Mulligan

THE ROLLING STONES

A Musical Biography

Murry Nelson

THE STORY OF THE BAND
CHRIS SMITH, SERIES EDITOR

GREENWOOD

AN IMPRINT OF ABC-CLIO, LLC
Santa Barbara, California • Denver, Colorado • Oxford, England

Library of Congress Cataloging-in-Publication Data

Nelson, Murry R.
  The Rolling Stones : a musical biography / Murry Nelson.
    p. cm. — (Story of the band)
  Includes bibliographical references and index.
  ISBN 978-0-313-38034-1 (alk. paper) — ISBN 978-0-313-38035-8 (ebook)
  1. Rolling Stones.   2. Rock musicians—England—Biography.   I. Title.
  ML421.R64N45   2010
  782.42166092'2—dc22
  [B]   2010014753

ISBN: 978-0-313-38034-1
EISBN: 978-0-313-38035-8

14   13   12   11   10   1   2   3   4   5

This book is also available on the World Wide Web as an eBook.
Visit www.abc-clio.com for details.

Greenwood
An Imprint of ABC-CLIO, LLC

ABC-CLIO, LLC
130 Cremona Drive, P.O. Box 1911
Santa Barbara, California 93116-1911

This book is printed on acid-free paper ∞

Manufactured in the United States of America

Contents

Series Foreword

Green Day! The Beatles! U2! The Rolling Stones! These are just a few of the many bands that have shaped our lives. Written for high school students and general readers, each volume in this exciting series traces the life of a band from its beginning to the present day. Each examines the early life and family of band members, their formative years and inspirations, their career preparation and training, and the band's awards, achievements, and lasting contributions to music.

Designed to foster student research, the series has a convenient format. Each book begins with a timeline that charts the major events in the life of the band. The narrative chapters that follow trace the birth, growth, and lasting influence of the band across time. Appendices highlight awards and other accomplishments, while a selected bibliography lists the most important print and electronic resources for high school student research—or for anyone just interested in learning more about the band.

These books also help students learn about social history. Music, perhaps more than any other force, has shaped our culture, especially in recent times. Songs comment on the events of their era and capture the spirit of their age. They powerfully touch the lives of listeners and help people—especially young people—define who they are. So too, the lifestyles of band members reflect larger social trends and promote and provoke reactions within society. By learning about the bands, students also learn more about the world they live in.

So have a seat, settle in, and crank up the volume!

Introduction

In July 1962 a musical group made its first appearance at the Marquee Jazz Club in London. It was not until early in 1963, however, that the entire band, consisting of Mick Jagger, Brian Jones (d. 1969), Keith Richards, Ian Stewart (d. 1985), Bill Wyman (née Perks), and Charlie Watts, who had missed the debut and a number of other shows through the rest of 1962, performed together on stage at the Ricky Tick Club in Windsor, Berkshire, outside London, playing rhythm and blues rather than jazz. After Brian Jones's death, Mick Taylor joined the group but left in 1974; Ron Wood joined the band in 1976. Bill Wyman left the band in 1993.

Bands were forming all over England at the time, and the success of the Beatles, from Liverpool, only accelerated those formations. Most of the bands didn't stay together long, or they just became casual performers on weekends. There was no initial reason to see these young men, ranging in age from 19 to 27, as any different from the many other bands. This new band, named the Rolling Stones by one of its founders, Brian Jones, might have just become like so many other bands but for their luck, tenacity, and musical talent. They chose to play more rhythm and blues, which made them less popular with most of the jazz club owners. They also decided, first as individuals and later as a group, to spend long hours practicing their music, leaving little time for real jobs.

By 1964 the United States had welcomed a number of British bands to American soil as the so-called British invasion began, led first by the Beatles and later by the Searchers, the Animals, Peter and Gordon, Chad and Jeremy, Herman's Hermits, Manfred Mann, the Who, and many more lesser known groups. The Rolling Stones came to the United States in June 1964 as the second most popular band in England, though they were much less well known in the United States. They returned in October to much more renown, and they soon established themselves in the United States as well as the United Kingdom as a musical phenomenon.

The band was seen as rowdier and more rebellious than the Beatles, the bad boys to the good boys, and this reputation was soon exploited by the Rolling Stones to enhance their popularity with their teenage fan base. The group released two record albums in the United States in 1964, with the first rising to number 11 and the second to number 3 on the U.S. musical charts. The Rolling Stones had set a foundation and proceeded to build on it. Unlike many bands, as noted, they stayed together, continued to improve, and expanded their musical repertoire.

Within five years, the Rolling Stones were the kings of rock and roll. The Beatles had stopped touring in 1966 and broke up in 1970, after most other British groups had also disbanded. The Rolling Stones, however, not only continued but flourished. Their tours drew thousands, though they continued to court controversy with their songs and actions. The tragic concert at Altamont, California, in December 1969 seemed to signal an end to the era of peace, love, and rock music. But that turned out not to be the case, as least as far as the Rolling Stones were concerned. Their eight albums, released from 1971 to 1981, all achieved number 1 status on the American music charts, and their nine band tours during that same period were also wildly popular, selling out at almost every venue in the United States, Europe, and Canada. At times, their entire lives seemed to be spent on the road.

Nearly thirty years later, after many rumors of a band breakup, the Rolling Stones are still the most popular band in the world. They have been together for more than 45 years, and they are still playing with passion and show no signs of letting up. The Rolling Stones have had albums of the year, been voted band of the year, were inducted into the Rock and Roll Hall of Fame (1989), have had three of the four largest grossing music tours in history, and have nothing left to prove. Yet they continue to play together because they love to do so. As of 2010, their future interest in touring and recording remains unclear, but their status as music legends is assured.

Acknowledgments

Every book requires the assistance of others, and this book was no exception. Kristi Ward, my initial editor, suggested and secured the project, while George Butler carried the project through as editor. Their help, particularly that of George, was most vital to the work. The librarians at Penn State University assisted me in obtaining books through interlibrary loan. A number of readers reviewed all or part of the manuscript, and I thank David Skinner, Jake Edmondson, and my wife, Elizabeth Nelson, for their patience in this aspect of the work. Jackie Edmondson provided suggestions and useful discussions on the nature of writing biographies of musicians. Reviewers from the It's Only Rock and Roll Web site posted useful reviews for many of the concerts that the Stones had performed over the years. I appreciate their details and insight.

Of course, any mistakes are my own fault, as are the conclusions made in the work. It has been a great pleasure writing about the Rolling Stones, and I would be remiss in not acknowledging the inspiration and pleasure that their music has provided to me over the years.

Timeline

October 24, 1936	William George Perks (Bill Wyman) is born in London.
July 18, 1938	Ian Stewart is born in Pittenweem, Fife, Scotland.
June 2, 1941	Charles Robert Watts is born in London.
February 28, 1942	Lewis Brian Hopkin-Jones is born in Cheltenham.
July 26, 1943	Michael Philip Jagger is born in Dartford.
December 18, 1943	Keith Richards is born in Dartford.
June 1, 1947	Ronald David Wood is born in Yiewsley (Hillingdon).
January 17, 1949	Michael Kevin Taylor is born in Hatfield.
November 1961	Keith Richards joins Little Boy Blue and the Blue Boys Band, formed by Mick Jagger, Dick Taylor, Bob Beckwith, and Allen Etherington.
March 17, 1962	Brian Jones hears Alexis Korner's Blues Incorporated play at Ealing Jazz Club, London. The drummer is Charlie Watts. Jones introduces himself to Korner.
March 24, 1962	Jones plays with Blues Incorporated at Ealing Jazz Club.
April 7, 1962	Jagger and Richards hear Blues Incorporated (with Jones and Watts) at Ealing Jazz Club. Jones, Richards, and Jagger meet and talk after the set.

April 21, 1962	Jagger, Richards, and Dick Taylor play a guest spot at Ealing Jazz Club with Blues Incorporated, including Charlie Watts.
May 1962	Brian Jones places an ad in *Jazz News* seeking players for a new R&B band. Among respondents is Ian Stewart, who becomes part of the new nameless band.
May 25, 1962	Jagger, Richards, and Dick Taylor visit Bricklayer's Arms pub, where Jones and his band are rehearsing.
June 1962	Jagger and Richards join Jones, Stewart, Dick Taylor, and Geoff Bradford in the band. A number of drummers are tried.
July 12, 1962	First gig of the new band, dubbed the Rolling Stones, is held at Marquee Jazz Club, London. The group consists of Jagger, Richards, Jones (Elmo Lewis), Stewart, Taylor, and Mick Avory on drums.
December 1962	Bill Wyman hears the Stones play at Red Lion pub and is invited to rehearsals because they need a bass player to replace Dick Taylor.
December 15, 1962	Bill Wyman plays his first gig with the Rolling Stones at Youth Club, Church Hall, London.
January 1963	Charlie Watts sits in with the band at some gigs, before officially agreeing to become a member of the Rolling Stones in mid-January.
February 24, 1963	First appearance at Crawdaddy Club, Station Hotel, Richmond.
May 6, 1963	Rolling Stones sign a management contract with Andrew Loog Oldham and Eric Easton, who had heard them at the Crawdaddy Club within the previous week. A recording contract is signed three days later.
May 8, 1963	Ian Stewart is informed that he is out of the group, based on Oldham's view of Stewart's image. He is invited to be road manager and play in studio recordings and accepts the offer.
May 14, 1963	Decca Records agrees to contract with Impact Sound (Easton and Oldham).
June 7, 1963	First single, "Come On," is released in England.
November 1, 1963	Second single, "I Wanna Be Your Man" (John Lennon and Paul McCartney, writer/composer), is released.

March 6, 1964	First U.S. single, "Not Fade Away," is released.
May 2, 1964	First album, *The Rolling Stones*, is released in England and goes to number 1 on the charts.
May 29, 1964	First U.S. album, *England's Newest Hitmakers—The Rolling Stones*, is released.
June 5, 1964	First U.S. tour begins in San Bernardino, California.
July 1964	Bill Perks changes his name to Bill Wyman.
October 25, 1964	First appearance on the *Ed Sullivan Show* while on their second American tour.
June 5, 1965	First number 1 hit in the United States, "Satisfaction," is released.
July 30, 1965	First album to reach number 1 in United States, *Out of Our Heads*, is released.
August 28, 1965	Stones sign a management agreement with Allen Klein.
April 15, 1966	First album to contain only Jagger/Richards songs, *Aftermath*, is released in the United Kingdom (U.S. release is two months later).
June 24, 1966	Fifth U.S. tour opens in Lynn, Massachusetts. This is the final U.S. tour for Brian Jones.
February 12, 1967	Infamous drug bust at Redlands, home of Keith Richards, results in arrests of Richards, Mick Jagger, Marianne Faithfull, and other acquaintances.
February 25, 1967	Brian Jones is hospitalized in Toulouse, France, while on the road to Morocco with Keith Richards and Anita Pallenberg, where they are to meet Mick Jagger and Marianne Faithfull.
June 27, 1967	Mick Jagger is found guilty of drug charges. Keith Richards is convicted two days later, and both are sentenced to fines and imprisonment. Both are released on bail on June 30.
July 31, 1967	Richards's conviction is overturned and Jagger's is reduced on appeal to probation.
October 31, 1967	Brian Jones is convicted of drug charges and sentenced to prison but bonded the next day. The sentence is set aside and replaced by a fine on December 12.
May 12, 1968	Band makes a surprise appearance and plays at the *New Musical Express* Poll-Winners Concert. This is the last public appearance of Brian Jones.
December 10–12, 1968	*The Rolling Stones Rock 'n Roll Circus* is filmed but withheld from broadcast because the band is dissatisfied

	with the result. It is finally released on DVD in 1996.
June 1969	Mick, Keith, and Charlie visit Brian at his home at Cotchford Farm and tell him that he is being dropped from the band. He agrees to a settlement and issues a statement that he has resigned.
June 13, 1969	Mick Taylor is introduced as the newest member of Rolling Stones.
July 2 and 3, 1969	Brian Jones drowns in his pool at Cotchford Farm. His death is ruled "by misadventure" by the coroner.
July 5, 1969	Stones give a free concert in Hyde Park and call it a tribute to Brian Jones. It is their first concert in more than two years.
November 7, 1969	Rolling Stones open their first U.S. tour in over three years in Ft. Collins, Colorado.
December 6, 1969	The infamous Altamont free concert is held in the East Bay area of San Francisco. Filmed by the Maysles brothers as part of *Gimme Shelter,* the murder of a young man by Hell's Angels is the horrific highlight of the movie.
July 30, 1970	The Rolling Stones begin severance action against Allen Klein.
September 2, 1970	Stones begin their first European tour in three years in Helsinki, Finland.
April 6, 1971	Band signs a new record agreement with Atlantic Records and gets their own label, Rolling Stones Records.
April 23, 1971	First album on Rolling Stones Records, *Sticky Fingers,* is released.
May 10, 1972	The Rolling Stones and Allen Klein issue a statement that they have settled their differences. Ultimately, the Stones pay off Klein and give him rights to their pre-1970 material.
January 18, 1973	The Stones perform a benefit concert for victims of the devastating late December Nicaraguan earthquake. Mick Jagger had earlier chartered a plane and flown vaccines into Managua, capital of Nicaragua and hometown of Bianca Jagger.
July 31, 1973	Fire at Redlands, Keith Richards's home, ravages the structure, but Keith, Anita, and their children emerge unscathed.

December 13, 1974	Mick Taylor officially resigns from the Stones. He had informed the band two weeks before.
April 14, 1975	Stones announce that Ron Wood of Faces will join the band, but only for the upcoming U.S. tour (June–August).
February 28, 1976	Ron Wood is announced as an official member of the Rolling Stones.
January 12, 1977	Keith Richards found guilty of possession of cocaine and LSD in court north of London. He is fined about $1,500 and costs of about $500.
February 16, 1977	Stones agree to a new worldwide record distribution deal with EMI, but a North American distributor is not announced. In April Atlantic Records is announced as that distributor.
February 27, 1977	Police raid Keith and Anita's hotel rooms at the Harbour Castle Hotel and confiscate a large amount of heroin and cocaine. Keith is charged with trafficking and possession.
March 4, 1977	Stones play in El Mocambo, a small Toronto club, with Prime Minister Trudeau's wife in attendance. She parties with them afterward at their hotel.
April 1, 1977	Keith is allowed to leave Canada and enter the United States to undergo treatment for heroin addiction.
May 14, 1978	Bianca Jagger files for divorce after seven years of marriage. By this time Mick has become ensconced with Jerry Hall, whom he had met two years earlier.
October 24, 1978	Keith, after plea bargaining, is sentenced to one year suspended sentence and to give a benefit concert for the blind as punishment for the possession of heroin plea in Toronto.
April 22, 1979	Two benefit concerts are held in Oshawa, Ontario.
December 18, 1979	Keith meets model Patti Hansen in New York City at his 36th birthday party. They marry four years later, on December 18.
August 26, 1981	Stones announce first U.S. tour in three years, to run September to December.
July 25, 1982	Last concert of European tour is held in Yorkshire. The Stones will not tour again for seven years.
July 13, 1985	Live Aid for Africa concert is broadcast from Philadelphia and London. In Philadelphia Mick Jagger plays solo backed by Hall and Oates, then with Tina

	Turner. Keith Richards and Ron Wood play with Bob Dylan to close the show.
December 12, 1985	Ian Stewart dies of a heart attack in London at age 47. All the Stones attend his funeral a week later.
November 24, 1988	Keith Richards opens a tour in Atlanta with his new band, the X-Pensive Winos. They do 15 shows in 23 days.
January 18, 1989	The Rolling Stones are inducted into the Rock and Roll Hall of Fame at a function in the Waldorf Astoria Hotel in New York.
March 15, 1989	Rolling Stones sign a deal to do their first tour in seven years, beginning in August. Guarantee is $70 million for the Steel Wheels Tour
February 1990	Rolling Stones tour Japan for the first time.
November 19, 1991	Stones agree to a record deal with Virgin Records, the largest record agreement in history.
January 6, 1993	Bill Wyman makes the official announcement of his retirement from the Rolling Stones.
November 1993	Final recording of new album, *Voodoo Lounge,* is done in Dublin. Darryl Jones plays bass and subsequently becomes the new bass player of the band; however, he is not a full member of the Stones but rather an employee.
August 1994–1995	Voodoo Lounge Tour plays North America, South America, South Africa, Japan, Australia, New Zealand, and Europe. It grosses over $320 million, the highest-grossing tour to that date.
October 15, 1996	*The Rolling Stones Rock'n Roll Circus* from December 1968 is released on VHS and subsequently DVD.
August 1997	The Stones announce a new tour, Bridges to Babylon, which will coincide with the new album of the same name. The tour opens on September 4 and runs through September 1998, including an additional short European section in June 1999. The tour plays to 4.6 million people and grosses over $300 million.
August 11, 1998	The Rolling Stones play for the first time in Russia, before 83,000 fans in Moscow.
May 2002	Rolling Stones meet in Paris to record new songs for the *40 Licks* album, celebrating 40 years together. The 40 Licks Tour, to run from September 2002 to November 2003, is announced in New York City.

December 12, 2003	Mick Jagger is knighted by Prince Charles. Announced in the summer of 2002, Jagger had been too busy to attend a ceremony until 2003.
June 2005	Mixes for *A Bigger Bang* album are completed, and the new Bigger Bang Tour, to run from August 2005 to August 2007, is announced.
February 18, 2006	The Stones give a free concert on Copacabana Beach in Rio de Janeiro, Brazil, before more than one million fans.
April 8, 2006	Rolling Stones play first ever concert in mainland China, in Shanghai.
April 27, 2006	Keith Richard falls out of a coconut tree in Fiji and suffers head trauma and brain damage. He is flown to New Zealand for cranial surgery, recovers, and the Bigger Bang Tour resumes in July in Italy.
July 28, 2007	Rolling Stones perform at Palace Square, outside the Winter Palace in St. Petersburg, Russia.
August 23, 2007	Bigger Bang Tour ends after playing in 32 countries and grossing more than $558 million, the largest tour sales ever.

CHAPTER ONE

The Young Stones

Young Bill Perks

The bombs began to fall on London in early September 1940. The Nazi blitzkrieg was designed not only to destroy property and people but also to crush the will to fight, to convince Britain to surrender to the German onslaught before the country was destroyed.

The bombing was not unexpected; it was a matter of when it would begin. Anticipating the attacks on the capital, thousands of women and children were evacuated to the countryside, usually to the homes of relatives or sympathetic countrymen. That was the case with young William Perks Jr. (b. October 24, 1936), the oldest child of William and Kathleen (known as Molly), who accompanied his mother and two siblings to Pembrokeshire, Wales, in April 1940. Bill's mother was lonely and unhappy in Wales, however, and the brood returned to London a few weeks later to become observers/victims of the Battle of Britain, which raged in the skies above England from July through October 1940.

Bill remembered gazing at the skies above London as waves of German bombers crossed from occupied France to England for their bombing runs and to be attacked by the British Royal Air Force fighter planes. It was an exciting and dangerous time. Many nights the family slept in their back garden air-raid shelter, as did thousands of other Britons. Extended families were thrown together for safety; commercial buildings and homes were destroyed by the seemingly ceaseless bombing raids. After October, the regular nightly raids ended, but bombing runs still continued through May 1941. At that point, it was clear to the Germans that there would be no British surrender and that the continued raids were futile. Nevertheless sporadic raids went on for years until the end of World War II in 1945.

Much of Great Britain, particularly the important cities, was reduced to rubble. By the end of May 1941, over 43,000 civilians, half of them in London, had been killed by bombing, and more than a million houses had been destroyed or damaged in London alone. London had a population of about 9 million people at the start of the war. Near the end of the war, Germany developed and launched V1 bombs and V2 rockets, which increased the death and destruction throughout England, most notably in London. An additional 9,000 persons died in London from the V1 and V2 attacks.

Fires also destroyed large numbers of buildings, with the most notable fire occurring in May 1941. By the end of the war, destruction or significant damage had been done to the British Houses of Parliament, the British Museum, St. James Palace, and thousands of other sites.

Despite all this carnage and horrific damage, the optimism and ignorance of youth gave young Bill and many of his peers rose-colored glasses. They saw the excitement and fun of being British at the time but were hardly traumatized by the crumbling of the nation. Everyone was in the same predicament, so the country pulled together through these hard times and people simply went without so many things that were considered staples in later years. Food rationing was in effect, limiting meat, bread, fruits, and vegetables, among many items.

Bill's dad was sent to Nottingham, about 120 miles north of London in the Midlands region, to help in the building of aircraft hangars, and it was there that Bill first began school in September 1941, at the age of five. Bill was often ridiculed at school because of his Cockney accent, and he was generally unhappy there. Thus, in August 1942, he was sent back to London to live with his grandparents in Penge, a section of London in Bromley Borough. (London is composed of 32 such boroughs.) Bill and his grandparents lived with Bill's aunt and a boarder in a small two-bedroom house with the toilet outside in the back garden. At this time, indoor plumbing was not found in many homes throughout the country.

In 1943 Bill and his family were reunited in their London home in Syndenham in the London borough of Lewisham, when his father was posted there. It was there that Bill first heard a radio and was immediately taken by the music of American swing musicians like Harry James, Glenn Miller, and Frank Sinatra. Bill had taken some piano lessons but now heard a different kind of music that energized him. In April the family moved to a new flat in Penge, and Bill attended junior school. And the war went on, often with frightening and very close encounters with bombs.

By the end of the war in 1945, Bill had seen destruction, knew classmates who had died in bombings, had suffered food shortages, and had discovered girls. The end of the war did not mean an end to shortages, though. Britain, like most of Europe, was a devastated nation, and the economy would take years to recover. In addition, some of the worst weather in British history kept conditions difficult. In 1947 the worst winter in modern British history was recorded in London, where snowdrifts 14 feet high were not uncommon. Work, travel, and commerce were nearly impossible, and life was difficult. Bill's dad took on other jobs, and his mother did small jobs within the house for cash like peeling onions for a local pickling company. All the children pitched in on this.

In September 1947, Bill was one of only three of his class of 52 to gain admittance and a scholarship to a prestigious grammar school, where he stood out for his athletic prowess, his scholarship, and his poverty. He continued his piano lessons and added clarinet lessons the next year. In May 1949 he passed his primary examinations on piano at the Royal College of Music in London.

Bill's chief interests in the early 1950s were music and girls. In the former category, his musical influences were largely American because British popular music was bland and uninspiring. American jazz, rhythm and blues (R&B), and the remnants of swing music were his favorites, mostly heard on Radio Luxembourg, a superstation, which was infinitely preferable to the boring tunes of the British Broadcasting Corporation (BBC). Bill heard the early electric guitar music of Les Paul and was intrigued by that. The bluesy, wailing sound of Johnny Ray's singing also captivated him.

In 1953 war rationing on sweets ended, and that was very popular among young people. In addition, a British Top 20 began, which indicated an increased interest in popular music. Bill was working to improve his weak areas in school, but his father decided that the family needed him to work, and his dad had him withdrawn from grammar school in March. Bill was disappointed in this, but his father made the decision and that was that. Now he sought work.

Bill's first job was as a junior clerk in a betting parlor (legal in England) in central London. He purchased a record player, began going to jazz clubs, and dreaded his call-up to military service after his 18th birthday, which was in October. He was called up in January 1955 and joined the Royal Air Force as a clerk. After signing up for extended service, he was posted to Germany in summer 1955. Bill and his mates listened to American Armed Forces Radio and first heard Chuck Berry, Bill Haley, Fats Domino, and Elvis Presley. These would be his music idols, the artists after whom he would initially pattern his guitar playing, which began after he bought a cheap secondhand guitar while on leave in Spain in summer 1956. In January 1957 Bill was assigned to the military transport section and got to know Lee Whyman, a fellow serviceman, much better. He admired Lee's style and his name and, after being discharged from the service, began calling himself Bill Wyman. (He legally changed his name in 1964.)

In late 1957, still in the Royal Air Force, Bill started a skiffle (a kind of folk music with jazz, blues, and country influences) group, and shortly after that, he finished his duty with the military. He returned to Penge, got a job in the offices of a meat importer, and met a girl at the Ballroom in Penge named Diane Maureen Cory. They dated and later married in October 1959. Bill was 23 and Diane 18.

Just over a year later, Bill changed jobs and, at his new job, met Steve Carroll, who played the guitar. Bill bought an electric guitar on an installment plan. Together with Cliff Starkey, his sister's brother-in-law, the three formed a group. A few months later, in late 1960, Bill went into more debt, purchasing an amplifier on installment. Beginning in January 1961, the group played gigs around the region at clubs, weddings, and house parties. They were getting paid, though not very much, and maintained their regular jobs but practiced a few times a week. They added a drummer, Tony Chapman, and a name for the group, the Cliftons. In August 1961, Bill and Diane attended a concert where he heard a group with a bass player. He realized that that was what the Cliftons were missing. He also felt that bass playing fit his personality since he didn't feel that he should be a front man, such as a lead guitarist or singer, but rather belonged in the background, where the drummer and bassist played. Bill returned home, bought a bass guitar, and practiced it in all his free time.

By January 1962, the Cliftons' sound was much tighter, and they were sounding like a real professional group.

Lewis Brian Hopkin-Jones

Brian Jones was born on February 28, 1942, and was raised in Cheltenham by his parents, both of whom enjoyed music greatly. His mother, Louisa, was a piano teacher, and his father, Lewis, an electrician's assistant who later became an aeronautical engineer, played piano and organ, and led his church choir. Cheltenham was one of the "gray ladies," an old town known for its spa and its traditional ways. Brian attended local schools and was an excellent student. He was admitted to Cheltenham Grammar School for Boys after passing his 11 Plus exams. Young Brian continued to excel and received piano training from his mother, while also mastering the clarinet by the age of 14. His musical talent seemed quite advanced, and he picked up various instruments easily, most notably the saxophone.

In 1957 he passed all of his O Level examinations, putting him on a path to an excellent university career. Jones, however, seemed to be interested less and less in academics, other than music, and more and more in girls. Brian was playing in a skiffle group, a popular form of music in England at the time, and began frequenting local jazz clubs, soon starting his own jazz group and playing in these same clubs. In 1959 his girlfriend became pregnant, and Brian urged her to have an abortion. Instead she had the child and gave it up for adoption. The scandal, combined with Jones's lack of interest in school, led him to drop out and leave England to tour through parts of the Continent. He had his guitar and saxophone, both of which served him well, as he got by playing music on the streets of Scandinavia for money (and also picking up girls). After a few months away he returned to Cheltenham in November 1959, broke but happy.

In January 1960 Brian began dating Pat Andrews, with whom he had a three-year, on-and-off relationship, and one child, a son whom he named Julian after the great jazz saxophonist, Julian "Cannonball" Adderly. Brian was also dating other women and had a brief affair with a married woman, which also led to a child. Brian took almost no responsibility for these children and was barely getting by working in factories and playing in various jazz clubs. Some of the jazz clubs brought in American blues artists; Brian became intrigued by blues music and sought records by Howlin' Wolf, Muddy Waters, Robert Johnson, and other lesser known blues musicians. Brian was still always short of cash and took on jobs as a city bus driver, a sales assistant, and a coalman but never held them for long.

In late 1961 Brian and his friend and bandmate Dick Hattrell went to the Cheltenham town hall to hear a concert by one of the first blues bands in Britain, the Chris Barber Band. The concert was billed as jazz, but one interval set was filled by Alexis Korner and Cyril Davies, later seen as the fathers of blues in England. Since blues music is an American invention with roots in African slave music, there was no base of such music in England. After the show, Brian went backstage and talked to Korner about Brian's enthusiasm for blues music, and Korner invited Brian and Dick to visit him when they were in London. In December 1961 Jones took up Korner on his offer and traveled to London for a few days, listening to live music as well as Korner's extensive record collection. Inspired by the music of Elmore James, Jones returned to Cheltenham and bought his first electric guitar, which he played for hours, seeking to master the techniques of slide guitar, a style that varies the string tone's length and pitch. In March 1962 Korner informed Brian that he had persuaded the Ealing Jazz Club in London to allow a rhythm and blues night, and Korner's group, Blues Incorporated, would be the debut act. Brian and Dick Hattrell hitchhiked to London for the opening on March 17.

A week later, at Korner's second session at the Ealing Jazz Club, Brian sat in with Blues Incorporated. It was at that point that he first met the drummer of the group, a 20-year-old graphic designer named Charlie Watts.

Charlie Watts

Charles Robert Watts was born on June 2, 1941, in London, to Charles Richard and Lillian Charlotte Watts. Even at a young age, when bombs were falling near his house and the family had to flee to the air-raid shelters, Charlie was a calm child. He remained that way, never too high or too low. His parents moved to another section of London in 1948, one that was still relatively green and semirural, and he began secondary school in 1952, displaying an early aptitude for art. In 1955, at 14, Charlie bought a banjo but was frustrated by his inability to play it correctly. He took it apart and played the skin, now set up on a stand, with brushes, his first drum set. That Christmas, his parents gave him a real drum kit, which he played to jazz records endlessly. Until joining the Rolling Stones, he had never listened to rock and roll.

In 1957, at 16, Watts left school with an O-Level certificate in art. Shortly afterward, he enrolled at Harlow School of Art. In 1960 he began work at an advertising agency, learning the basics of applied graphic design. He continued to sit in with various jazz groups and study jazz techniques from recordings. Intrigued by Charlie "Bird" Parker, the great jazz saxophonist, he wrote a book on him in 1961, which was published in 1965, after the Rolling Stones had become famous.

In 1961 Alexis Korner invited Watts to join his band, but he declined and went, instead, to Denmark for a few months, as part of his work for the design firm. On his return in early 1962, Korner reiterated his invitation, and Charlie accepted and became part of Korner's new band with Cyril Davies, Blues Incorporated. The music was more than jazz and wasn't rhythm and blues; rather it was an amalgam, not always predictable but exciting. Around this time Charlie met and later married Shirley Ann Shepherd, a student in sculpture at the Royal College of Art. So it was in March 1962 when Brian Jones first interacted with Charlie Watts.

By the next week, the band had expanded to include a new bass player, Jack Bruce. Brian was excited about the new sounds that they were mastering and the audience reactions, which were enthusiastic. Charlie was very positive about it also, but in his own, low-key manner. He and Jack Bruce hit it off and decided to rent a flat together and began playing on other nights besides at the Ealing Jazz Club. Sometimes another drummer, Ginger Baker, would sit in also. (In July 1966, Baker, Bruce, and Eric Clapton would form the group Cream, the first supergroup.) Blues Incorporated played their now regular performance at the Ealing Jazz Club on Saturday, April 7, and Korner introduced a new guest, Elmo Lewis (a sometime pseudonym used by Brian Jones, a paean to Elmore James and a bow to Brian's real first name.) In the audience that evening were 18-year-old Michael Jagger, a student at the London School of Economics and blues aficionado, and Keith Richards, also 18. Jagger and Richards were playing music regularly (though not publicly), and both were totally enthralled over Lewis's playing of the slide electric guitar, something they had never seen before. At that time Jones said that he was forming a band, and Jagger and Richards wanted to be involved.

Mick Jagger

Michael Philip Jagger was born July 26, 1943, in Dartfort, Kent, about 18 miles from London. Since 1849 Dartfort was connected to London via commuter train and was largely a bedroom community. Michael's father, Basil "Joe" Fanshawe Jagger, was a physical education teacher and rather a tyrant, despite his small size. Michael's mother, Eva Ensley Scutts Jagger, was a hairdresser, born in Australia, who came to England as a teenager. Michael was their first child, and another son, Christopher, was born in 1947. Young Michael went to Maypole Primary Infants School beginning in September 1947 and moved on to Wentworth Junior County Primary School in September 1950. On that same block in Dartfort lived young Keith Richards, also born in 1943, and the two first met in school in February 1951. Though not great friends, the two did know each other, and each recognized the other when they became reacquainted in 1960.

In 1954 the Jagger family moved to a larger home in Wilmington, about five miles away. In September 1954, Mike began at Dartford Grammar School, where he was a good, though not exceptional, pupil. He was exceptional, however, in his devotion to music. He would sit and listen to the radio for hours, then sing the songs that he had heard almost exactly in tone and inflection, according to his mother.[1] In the mid-1950s he bought his first guitar, when the family was on holiday in Spain. Mike was exposed to rhythm and blues music from the States for the first time when he took a job (at the age of 12) teaching physical education to American GI children at an army base near his home. His father's regimented physical education demands on Mike and his brother easily carried over into Mike's instructions to these younger children. Mike befriended an American cook at the base who had lots of R&B records, and young Mike was amazed by the sounds.

From then on, Mike played music and joined with his friend, Dick Taylor, in both jazz and skiffle groups. They were the typical garage band, playing all the radio tunes they heard. They called themselves the Blue Boys, and the band had Taylor, Jagger, and two friends, Bob Beckwith and Allen Etherington. They played Muddy Waters, Chuck Berry, Little Richard, Howlin' Wolf, and Bo Diddley tunes, among others. In 1959, in a basketball game (a sport in which Jagger had skill but in which he eventually lost interest), he crashed into another player, leading with his jaw, and bit off the tip of his tongue. Blood spurted from his mouth, and before he knew it, Mike had swallowed the tip. Friends noted that he didn't talk for days, which also meant that his band didn't play for days since he was the singer. When he did rejoin the band, his voice was different, "coarser, grittier," said Dick Taylor, who thought it might have been the best thing that happened to Mick Jagger.[2]

Mike saw his future in business and, to that end, thought that attending the prestigious London School of Economics would be a great asset. He applied himself to his schoolwork, once again, after a year or more of indifference. His marks improved, and he excelled on his exams. On the basis of this and a begrudging recommendation from his headmaster, with whom he had a record of many disputes, Jagger was accepted into the London School of Economics with a partial state scholarship. The money was enough to pay for tuition, meaning that he would live at home and commute from Dartford. This initially suited him. Although rebellious, Jagger was always an obedient son, doing his physical exercise regimen at his father's behest and keeping his room neat.

At the London School, Jagger was a loner who came and went largely unnoticed by his classmates. After a time he began to linger in London, sometimes staying over with friends and engaging in lively discussions on arts and politics. It was at this time that he chose to drop being "Mike" and became "Mick." He continued his interest in blues music but was frustrated by the lack of interest in London shops to stock American blues records. One day he simply wrote to Chess Records in Chicago and asked how he could obtain various albums. They were happy to send records to him by mail, though it took a while for them to be received.

One day in October 1960, while waiting for the train at Dartford Station, he had an armful of his latest treasures, which he would play for his friends at the London School of Economics once he got to the city. Coincidentally, on that same platform, waiting for the train, was Keith Richards, his old acquaintance from Wentworth. They recognized each other, and Keith noticed the stack of records in Mick's arms. This piqued Keith's interest because he, too, loved American rhythm and blues music. They began to reminisce and talk about the records Mick had. Keith was eager to hear them, and they agreed to get together soon.

Keith Richards

Keith Richards was born in Dartford, Kent, on December 18, 1943. Keith was the only child of Herbert "Bert" William Richards, who worked at General Electric as a foreman, and Doris Maude Lydia Dupree Richards, who drove a bakery van during the war then sold washing machines. Doris's father was a musician who led a dance band in the 1930s and played guitar, fiddle, piano, and saxophone. Doris played the ukulele. Keith attended Westhill Infants School, then Wentworth Junior County Primary, where he first met Mike Jagger. Jagger recalled the first conversation they had. Keith was dressed in a cowboy outfit and Jagger asked him what he wanted to be when he grew up. Richards replied that he planned to be like Roy Rogers (an American singing cowboy and movie star) and play guitar.[3]

Mike's family moved to a newer, bigger home in Wilmington, and at about the same time, Keith's family moved to the other side of Dartford in 1955. From the age of two Keith exhibited a wonderful ability to sing almost any radio song by the likes of Frank Sinatra or Nat King Cole (well-known American crooners) and at the age of seven was given a saxophone, which he learned to play. Keith sang in school and church choirs, performing as a soloist with one choir in Westminster Abbey at Christmas.

In September 1956 Keith began at Dartford Technical College. He was, at best, an indifferent student, but for music. Music from America was slowly making its way across the Atlantic, and it was exciting for thousands of young English students, including Keith. Elvis Presley, Fats Domino, Little Richard, Chuck Berry, and Jerry Lee Lewis had the most impact. His parents bought him a record player in 1958, and he listened to as many records as he could get his hands on, despite the poor quality of the record player and the records themselves. On his 15th birthday, in 1958, he received an acoustic guitar, and he began to practice, seemingly nonstop. Except for a few chords, initially taught by his grandfather, Keith is self-taught.

At 16 Keith was asked to leave Dartford Technical School because of his truancy. He was enrolled in Sidcup Art School and took a course in advertising. For the next three years he took a number of courses in graphic design and drawing, but mainly he played guitar. There were, he said, a lot of other guitar players at art school.[4] These included Dick Taylor and Michael Ross, and the three formed a country and western band.

After running into Mick Jagger at the Dartford train station, Keith joined him and Dick Taylor in playing together regularly at Mick's house. After joining with Keith and Dick, Mick played the guitar less and focused more on harmonica and singing. The practice moved to Dick Taylor's house in late 1961, where the three were joined by Allen Etherington on maracas and Bob Beckwith on guitar.

The boys decided that they needed a name, and they settled on Little Boy Blue and the Blue Boys.

The Boys Form a Band

In March 1962 the boys read about the Ealing Jazz Club in *Jazz News* and attended the performance on April 7, 1962, where Elmo Lewis (Brian Jones) first met Keith Richards and Mick Jagger. Before that the Blue Boys had sent a tape to Alexis Korner of some of their best work, and Korner was impressed with their sound, particularly Mick's singing. He called Mick and invited him to come by and visit, which he did, with Keith. Mick and Keith became inseparable once they found how much they had in common regarding their musical tastes, dreams, and abilities. Soon Keith and Mick were jamming with Blues Incorporated at some of their sets at the Ealing Jazz Club, though often it was only Mick invited to participate. Still, neither of them had any ideas about a real career in music, unlike Brian Jones.

Jones felt that he could and would become a professional blues musician, and he tried to recruit members for his intended band. A number of musicians turned him down, thinking that such a band would never be successful in England. To further his intentions, Brian moved to a cheap flat in West Hempstead, London. Brian was later surprised by the unexpected visit of Pat Andrews with their baby son Julian. She moved in with Brian. Shortly thereafter they were forced by the landlord to move because of the baby's presence, and they found another flat in the Notting Hill Gate area of London. Pat worked in a laundry, then as a computer-tape operator, while Brian took a sales job in the sports department of a department store. They made little, and Brian spent a lot on going out to visit clubs.

Brian put a small ad in *Jazz News* seeking band members, and a keyboardist named Ian Stewart was the first respondent. Stewart was an export sales clerk in a department store. He was a very knowledgeable musician, but the American blues were not very familiar to him. He joined Jones in rehearsing with a number of would-be band members, mostly recruited by Alexis Korner. Two guitarists, Geoff Bradford and Brian Knight, became regulars with the band. Mick Jagger, who had been singing with Blues Incorporated three nights a week during early spring 1962, quit them to join Brian and Ian's band. Shortly thereafter, Keith Richards and Dick Taylor were part of the new band, which rehearsed two nights a week.

The band was searching for the right songs and rhythms on which they all agreed and enjoyed playing. Chuck Berry, Muddy Waters, Bo Diddley, and Jimmy Reed seemed to be the artists whom they almost all liked the best and whose songs they focused on playing. Geoff Bradford was a real blues purist and was not able to accept playing these artists, almost exclusively, and he left the band.

The band was sounding good, but there were holes, the most notable of which was the lack of a drummer. Brian's first choice was Charlie Watts, playing with Blues Incorporated, but Charlie liked playing with Korner and still saw his future in graphic design, not music, so he refused the invitation. Brian put out another ad, this time in *Melody Maker,* for a drummer, and Tony Chapman, who had been part of Bill Wyman's group the Cliftons, answered the ad and joined the band, though some of the members didn't find his playing good enough.

Charlie Watts was playing in three bands when Brian asked him to join the Rolling Stones and replace Tony Chapman, who had only been a fill-in. Charlie went to a rehearsal, where he first met Bill Wyman, who, according to Keith, was only there initially because he had a couple big amplifiers. For a short time Charlie also lived with Mick, Brian, and Keith at a flat in Edith Grove, where they all became a real band, simply through their closeness and shared goal of success at being a band.

Charlie's limited exposure to R&B was expanded by playing with Brian, Keith, and Mick and by listening to the many R&B records they had. Of great significance to the band was the playing of Jimmy Reed, an American blues singer and guitarist who was an early proponent of electric blues and the intersection of two lead guitars. Most times there were lead, bass, and rhythm guitars, but Reed's playing got Brian and Keith to interweave their guitar work and excited Charlie Watts in his playing.

In July 1962 the band (still unnamed) got a break when Alexis Korner's Blues Incorporated were invited to play on the BBC's highly regarded (and listened to) radio show *Jazz Club.* To accept the spot, Korner's band would have to skip their regular Thursday night location, the Marquee, and the owner of the club there told them that if they accepted, he wouldn't guarantee them a return engagement. In addition, there was only room for six members, so Jagger stepped down from the engagement. Korner suggested a compromise that was accepted. Jagger, Jones, Stewart, Taylor, and Richards would play at the Marquee along with a drummer, who they would recruit (and who turned out to be Mick Avory, who subsequently joined the Kinks in 1964 and played with them until 1984). Before the appearance at the Marquee Club, the group needed a name. Despite the fact that Mick was seen as the lead of the group, it was Brian's group, and he decided that they should be the Rollin' Stones, after a favorite Muddy Waters song. Some of the members hated it (Ian Stewart, for one), and others were indifferent, but the name stuck. On Thursday, July 12, 1962, the Rolling Stones (the *g* was added almost immediately) made their first public appearance at the Marquee Club. *Jazz News* announced the gig on July 11 and highlighted Mick as the R&B vocalist who would lead the group, which consisted of Keith Richards, Elmo Lewis (Brian), Dick Taylor (on bass), Ian Stewart, and Mick Avory. The band played 15 numbers and were cheered vigorously by some in the audience and roundly booed by the jazz purists. Nevertheless, they did elicit excitement, and the owner of the Marquee, Harold Pendleton, decided to keep them on regularly. The Rolling Stones began seeking other gigs, too, which led them, ultimately, to playing regularly at the Crawdaddy Club, located within the Station Hotel in Richmond, southwest London.

It was around this time (late summer 1962) that Brian and Keith pushed Mick into finally leaving home and moving into a two-bedroom apartment with the two of them in Edith Grove, in the Chelsea section of London. Keith had completed art school and refused to find a job. Brian kept quitting or getting fired and tried to get by on whatever small amount the boys made from playing. Mick was still enrolled at the London School of Economics, and the only steady income that the three had was from Mick's scholarship money. They had little in the flat and lived what might be charitably called a bohemian existence. They were pigs. There was a single lightbulb hanging in each room. The flat was never cleaned, and they left garbage strewn around the apartment: broken glasses, cigarette butts, half-eaten sandwiches, grimy clothes (which were never washed), and walls smeared with excrement and boogers, often signed and identified. Brian and Keith had never been known for their neatness, but Mick had been a neat freak at home, always tidying his room and dressing in well-maintained clothing. For a short time, Pat Andrews and baby Julian lived with them, but it became too much for her and she left. Whenever they were short on food, the older women in the apartment downstairs provided soup, and the young men would occasionally have casual sex with them as a kind of payment, according to Andersen.[5] The students in the flat above them had parties, and the boys would often slip into the upstairs apartment after all the attendees had passed out. Then Brian, Keith, and Mick would help themselves to whatever was left to eat, drink, and smoke. They would also gather the bottles and return them for the deposit money. They lived like derelicts.

For financial assistance, they took in other roommates. One was an old friend of Brian's who seemed devoted to Brian. In return, Brian, who was often cruel and sadistic, tormented him and drove him out from the apartment after a few weeks. Then came another roommate, Jimmy Phelge, whose habits were even more disgusting than the habits the boys were already practicing. After a few weeks, even they were disgusted by Phelge's conduct, and he moved on. They did retain the interest in his name, however, immortalized in the copyrighted ownership name for a number of their later songs (Nanker Phelge).

The winter was severely cold; they had few blankets and not enough money to feed the coin-operated electric heater on a regular basis, and they often slept together in one double bed for warmth. Mick, from high school, had loved dressing in drag or wearing makeup at times. This continued during this period and fed rumors of homosexual behavior among the three of them. Then, and later, they did little to dispel the rumors since it added to their bad-boy image, which brought them attention. The keen and constant interest that all three had in women, however, seems to belie such rumors. Most likely, there were homosexual acts, though details are always sketchy. Often these were used to hurt or take advantage of one another, more power than sexual games.[6] To amuse themselves, the boys often told dirty jokes and made bizarre faces at each other. One face that Brian perfected, in which his nose was turned up and his lower eyelids pulled down, was called the "nanker." Many of their songs would be copyrighted by their corporation, Nanker Phelge.

As for the band, drummers came and went, as did bassists. Only Brian, Keith, and Mick were constants. Dick Taylor returned to his studies. There weren't enough gigs, even though R&B music was becoming more popular. There weren't enough clubs, and the club owners weren't all enamored of blues music, so opportunities to play and make money were very limited.

In December 1962 the boys sought a bass guitarist, and Tony Chapman suggested a guy he knew named Bill Wyman. Wyman joined them for a rehearsal on December 7 at the Wetherby Arms and brought two large amplifiers. This was the real reason that he was asked to join the band, but his bass soon began fitting well into the sounds of the Rolling Stones. Still, Wyman was irregular because of family and work commitments, and Dick Taylor would still sit in on bass.

Charlie Watts soon became the regular drummer and, as noted, lived for a short time in Edith Grove. The band cut a demo record, in which no record company had an interest. On January 14, 1963, the band, consisting of Brian, Keith, Mick, Charlie, Ian Stewart, and Bill, played their first gig together at the Flamingo Club in Soho, London, though Bill used the name "Lee Wyman" and Brian was still calling himself "Elmo Lewis." That soon changed, and the Rolling Stones, organized and led by Brian Jones, became a reality.

NOTES

1. Bill Wyman, with Ray Coleman (1990), *Stone Alone: The Story of a Rock 'n Roll Band*, New York: Viking, p. 94.
2. Christopher Andersen (1993), *Jagger, Unauthorized*, New York: Delacorte Press, p. 32.
3. Wyman, *Stone Alone*, p. 95; Lorne Michaels (Director) (1988), *25 × 5: The Continuing Adventures of the Rolling Stones;* Philip Norman (1984), *Symphony for the Devil*, New York: Linden Press/Simon and Schuster; Mick Jagger, Keith Richards, Charlie Watts, and Ronnie Wood (2003), *According to the Rolling Stones*, ed. Dora Lowenstein and Philip Dodd, London: Weidenfeld and Nicolson, p. 23.
4. Wyman, *Stone Alone*, p. 27.
5. Andersen, *Jagger, Unauthorized*, p. 52.
6. Ibid., pp. 55–57.

CHAPTER TWO

The British Invasion

The Rolling Stones were still struggling to have regular engagements in the early part of 1963. Charlie and Bill were still working at their regular jobs, and Mick was still, technically, at the London School of Economics; all three figured they needed some real job to go through life, but the band was still something to which they were committed with the rest of their time. Only Brian and Keith were hoping that they would have a real future in music, and neither held a real job for long, if at all. Ian Stewart, the "sixth Rolling Stone," also remained in his regular job.

Getting bookings was difficult since there was still great prejudice among jazz club owners against rhythm and blues. A big break for the Stones came from Giorgio Gomelsky, the promoter of the Crawdaddy Club. Gomelsky came to England in 1955 at the age of 21, having been born in the Soviet Union (Georgia), and lived in Switzerland just before leaving the Continent. He had been able to listen to forbidden prewar jazz while hiding in a friend's attic during World War II, and he became a committed jazz aficionado. He also discovered blues late in the 1950s and had followed the visits of American bluesmen to England, like Big Bill Broonzy, Muddy Waters, and Memphis Slim (John Chatman). Gomelsky began playing blues, rather than skiffle, on his weekly jazz radio show. In the course of that he became well acquainted with Alexis Korner and Blues Incorporated and began regularly attending their Thursday night sessions at the Marquee Club. One evening, during a lengthy band break, a young man with a decided lisp overheard Gomelsky lamenting the lack of new blood and real energy in the music scene. The young man said that Gomelsky should hear *his* band. Of course, the young man was Brian Jones, and Gomelsky took him up on his offer.

Impressed by what he heard, Gomelsky sought a venue where such a rhythm and blues band could be seen and heard regularly. He found the Station Hotel in Richmond, the last stop on the Richmond underground line in southwest London. The back room of the pub became the Crawdaddy Club and, when a band dropped out at short notice, Gomelsky contacted Brian and booked the Stones for a Sunday night in February 1963. There was little publicity, and a rare London snowfall made travel challenging. Attendance was in single digits (Gomelsky said three, Bill Wyman claimed six), but the small numbers there were highly appreciative. Gomelsky promised each of them free admission the next week if they returned with two others. This continued for about a month, and attendance increased dramatically. It was aided by Gomelsky and the band, who posted fliers around a nearby art college. Many students came, and by spring the Crawdaddy Club had more than a hundred at the Stones' engagements. The Stones were making a small amount from these engagements, in contrast to their weekly appearances at the Ealing Jazz Club for the past few months, where they had received nothing.

Audiences were getting revved up about the Stones. Gomelsky helped. One evening he had one of his assistants start dancing on one of the small tables in the club, and soon the entire audience was on its feet, dancing. From week to week the size of the audience grew so that there was little room to dance anywhere but the tables. Meanwhile, the tiny stage was becoming a dance floor for Mick's spinning, whirling, and head-shaking. The more the audience got involved, the more Mick gyrated, and all the Stones loved it. There was a youthful infectiousness to the performances that permeated everyone there. Many of the Stones saw this as the real crystallization of the band.

Gomelsky also managed to line up another series of engagements for the Rolling Stones, beginning Sunday, March 3, 1963, at the Ken Colyer Club, Studio 51, in Soho (a section of the center of London in the West End). Immediately after their playing in the afternoon, the group drove right to the Crawdaddy Club for their engagement there. The band played two sets of about 45 minutes each, beginning about 8 o'clock and finishing by about 10, with a half-hour break in between. As the audiences grew, the band noticed that there were some of the same faces at different venues. The Rolling Stones were developing a following, and fans were coming to hear *them*, not just R&B or because it was a convenient venue.

The pattern for each evening at the Crawdaddy Club was similar. In the first set, the band would play songs that they were first trying out and new arrangements of songs that they'd been playing. It was a glorified rehearsal of sorts. Then, after the 30 to 45 minute break, when everyone went to the bar, the Stones would return to a rowdier audience and play much more intensely. The driving beat would get people dancing, though as the crowds grew, there wasn't a lot of room, so many times the audience would just sway in place, arms waving rhythmically above their heads. By late spring, people were lined up at 2:00 P.M. to get into the place five hours later. Local and regional newspapers wrote stories about the popularity of the Stones and the Crawdaddy, which, ironically, led to the club being given notice by the hotel. Gomelsky moved the club to the grounds of the Richmond Athletic Association, where the Stones continued to pack in patrons for a time before moving on to touring and recording. The club also highlighted the Yardbirds, who also went on to greater fame.[1]

At this time British rock music was just becoming known, not just in Britain but also in North America. The Beatles had released their first number one hit in England, "Love Me Do," in late 1962, then "Please, Please Me," which hit the top of the British charts in February 1963. On April 14, Giorgio Gomelsky was at a London television studio where the Beatles were recording for an upcoming show. Gomelsky, who was also a filmmaker, was talking to the Beatles about doing a film with them and invited them to the Crawdaddy, just three miles away, to see the Rolling Stones later that night. Soon after the beginning of the first set, John, Paul, George, and Ringo appeared, dressed in identical long leather topcoats.

The Beatles loved the sound and the scene. The Stones were playing well; the fans were screaming and dancing on the tables. The walls shook and the atmosphere was entrancing. At the break the Beatles and Stones talked about their respective careers and ambitions. The Beatles then stayed for the entire second set, waited while the Stones packed their equipment, then accompanied the boys back to the Edith Grove flat, where they stayed for hours (until 4:00 A.M.), talking about music. They invited the Stones to their concert at the Royal Albert Hall the next Thursday, and the members of the groups promised to stay in touch. That Thursday, Brian, Keith, and Mick went to the Royal Albert Hall, where they carried in guitars owned by John, Paul, and George, allowing them to enter through the stage entrance. Some girls mistook them for Beatles and mobbed them. This set Brian off, saying things like, "This is what we want!" Still, there was conflict because Brian as well as the rest of the Stones had begun the band to spread the music, to make more converts to rock music. Now their idealism was being challenged by materialistic possibilities.

On Sunday, April 21, Giorgio had convinced the Stones that they should be the subjects of a short film (since he had failed to convince the Beatles to allow such a film to be made of them). The Stones rehearsed at a recording studio before coming to the Crawdaddy, where Giorgio filmed the late afternoon session. Gomelsky had also called a writer from *Record Mirror* and convinced him to attend the show. The next day the writer raved about the band to his colleagues and also to a young promoter, Andrew Loog Oldham, who had been working as a public relations assistant to Brian Epstein, the Beatles' manager. Oldham was immediately intrigued and contacted his partner/landlord, Eric Easton, a show business agent and manager who was 36 years old. Oldham was just 19 but was very savvy and energetic. He and Easton attended the Stones' performance in Richmond the next Sunday, where Oldham was overwhelmed and wanted to have some involvement with the Stones. Easton had reservations, however, feeling that Mick Jagger couldn't sing.

Oldham saw how sexy Brian and Mick were on stage and was enthralled by their raucous music and the response of the audience. He thought that the combination of sex and music was a surefire winner. He also saw, during the break, the rocky beginning of a three-year relationship that Mick would have with Chrissie Shrimpton, the 19-year-old younger sister of leading British model Jean "the Shrimp" Shrimpton. Chrissie and Mick had met two nights before when the Stones played at the Ricky Tick Club; at the break at the Crawdaddy the two were vehemently arguing in the alley, a pattern that would be a constant throughout their stormy relationship.

The next day Andrew contacted Brian Jones, and they met, along with Easton, at Easton and Oldham's office, where a three-year management contract was negotiated. Jones agreed to it then brought it around to Keith and Mick for their reaction, which was favorable, and the agreement was made on May 1, 1963, to begin on May 6. There were some demands, however. The most significant was that Ian Stewart would be dropped from the Stones at live performances.

Ian Stewart at the keyboard in 1971. (GETTY-85510355)

Oldham simply did not like his looks in relation to the rest of the band members. His hair was much shorter (to retain his job), and he had a prominent, oversized jaw, the result of a childhood illness that had made his jaw grow larger. Brian readily agreed to this, and none of the other Stones protested. Stewart was very hurt by the ouster, but Oldham said that he could still play in recording sessions and also be the band's road manager, which Stewart accepted reluctantly. Brian told Ian that he would always be a Rolling Stone and that they would be splitting their performance and recording income six ways. That was untrue.

On May 9 Brian signed a second contract with Andrew Oldham and Eric Easton, a three-year recording contract wherein the five Stones would receive a 6 percent royalty on all music sales. The band also retained control of their recordings, unlike the Beatles, whose recordings were controlled by their recording company, EMI/Capitol. This would prove profitable to the Stones and allow them the kind of control needed to further their own career as a band.

Giorgio Gomelsky had been out of the country during all this, following the death of his father in Switzerland. When he returned to London, he was both hurt and angry by what he felt was the betrayal of his work and an oral agreement to manage the Stones. They were unimpressed and began following the ambitious plans of Andrew Loog Oldham. He had contacted Decca Records and Dick Rowe, an executive there, who had gained infamy for turning down the Beatles as artists for Decca. He would not make such a mistake again. Interestingly, Rowe had been judging a music contest in Liverpool where one of the other judges was George Harrison, who urged Rowe to see the Stones perform and sign them up. After seeing them perform in Richmond and being impressed by the enthusiastic crowd reactions, Rowe did just that. Now the Stones had to decide what they would record for their first single. The result was "Come On," a Chuck Berry tune, and "I Want to Be Loved," a Muddy Waters song, as the B side. The single was released in June 1963.

To promote the band and the release of the single, Oldham secured a booking on the television show *Thank Your Lucky Stars,* where the band lip-synched to "Come On" while dressed in matching black-and-white blazers. As soon as the show ended, the band dumped the blazers in the garbage. Oldham had dressed them in these uniforms, like the Beatles, but it was not the Stones' persona, and he soon realized it. The Stones had longer, more unruly hair and were not as bubbly as the Beatles in appearance. The band was immediately embraced by teens, particularly girls, but also boys for their rebellious appearance and bad-boy image, which Oldham and the band cultivated. They were, in a sense, the anti-Beatles. Parents found their music and their appearance even more disgusting and threatening than the Beatles', and this made the Stones even more popular among British youth.

With recording, playing live, and rehearsing, the band was taking even more time each week than ever before. Bill and Charlie were struggling to keep up at their jobs, and there were times when Bill was forced to sneak off to a storeroom to sleep, with his absence covered by coworkers.[2] Charlie, who was still living with his parents, eventually quit to play full-time. Mick was still officially enrolled in the London School, but his appearances in class or on campus were becoming less and less frequent. Only Brian and Keith were almost totally jobless, banking on the band to provide income and direction. Initially they had hoped to become one of, if not the best, R&B rock band in London, but Andrew's vision was much loftier. He thought that they could transcend London and even England and be the best rock band in the world. His cockiness and confidence were infectious and changed the way the Stones looked at their own possible futures.

In August Bill quit his job to play bass full-time. The band was now working gigs Sunday afternoon, Sunday nights, and various venues and evenings, which was bringing them £25–55 per appearance. Mick, Brian, and Keith moved from their Edith Grove pigsty of a flat. Brian moved in with his current girlfriend, Linda Lawrence, and her parents, while Mick, Keith, and Andrew Oldham moved to a flat on Mapesbury Road in West Hempstead, London. Chrissie Shrimpton joined them as Mick's live-in girl, and he got her a job at Decca Records.

"Come On" rose to number 18 in the record charts, but the Stones hated it since it was not a real R&B song and was Andrew's choice because of its commercial appeal. Nevertheless, the band was getting publicity, lots of work, and had an upcoming fall tour scheduled by Andrew that included the American artists the Everly Brothers, Little Richard, and Bo Diddley. The Stones were excited about being with these American artists as well as the thrill of their first big tour through the United Kingdom. During the summer, Brian was often absent at gigs because of various ailments; he had asthma and also seemed very susceptible to any virus. The group either played with four or had Ian playing with his piano miked for it to be heard above the electric guitars.

The band was winding down its club dates and made farewell appearances at most of the regular spots like the Ken Colyer Club and the new Crawdaddy in Richmond. The band was preparing for its tour as well as seeking a follow-up record to "Come On." They went through a recording session but were dissatisfied with the way the songs sounded. They were feeling stymied, when Andrew happened to run into John Lennon and Paul McCartney in the Piccadilly section of London, where he explained the dilemma the Stones were facing. Paul and John said that they had a song for them and went with Andrew to where the Stones were rehearsing in Soho. After arriving there with Oldham, John and Paul played the song using the Stones' instruments. The band was delighted and thanked them for this gift, which was "I Wanna Be Your Man." The Stones practiced it, modified it to fit their sound, and recorded it. It became their next release and was perfectly timed for the tour of England that began September 29, 1963. The single was recorded on October 7, and the B side was a bit of improvisation that the boys made up on the spot, which they called "Stoned." It was the first thing they had written, and they liked the sound. The single was released on November 1.

Before that, however, the Stones agreed to open a charity concert that the Beatles were headlining at the Royal Albert Hall on September 15. Opening a concert is difficult because the audience is still getting settled in, and many are really there for just the headliners. But the Stones got the place rocking, with people out of their seats screaming. The Beatles were quite nervous because of the great audience response and hoped that they would not disappoint the excited audience. So despite their friendship, there was a bit of rivalry in the relationship between the Stones and the Beatles, one that was mostly flamed by the media rather than by the boys themselves.

The U.K. tour began in London and then traveled throughout England, places most of the Stones had never seen before. It lasted six weeks, and by the end the initial headliners, the Everly Brothers, had lost the top spot to Bo Diddley and the Stones. The tour ended on November 3, back in London, and the Stones had become quite polished in their performances as well as almost £1,300 richer for the 60 shows. It wasn't big money, but it indicated that the band could make a living as performers. The Stones learned a lot from all the American entertainers about performance, both on and off the stage. Mick watched the way Little Richard conducted himself, while Keith was amazed by Don Everly's chord work and playing techniques.

Charlie, Ian, and Bill had all quit their jobs, and Mick sent a letter of withdrawal to the London School of Economics just before the tour began. In addition, Bill was now being said to be 22 rather than his actual 27 since Andrew didn't think that any girls would be excited over an "old man" of 27. Bill was supposed not to be seen with his wife, and the other lads were told not to allow themselves to be photographed with their girlfriends since it would make them less appealing to their female fans, who could dream of dating or marrying a Rolling Stone. On the tour, there were often girls throwing themselves at the band members, and it was not uncommon for them to accept the offers of some of these young women and take them back to their hotel rooms for the night. The exception to all this action was Charlie Watts, who, according to band members, never engaged in this activity and remained totally faithful to his girlfriend and later wife, Shirley.[3]

As the tour ended, the Stones' second single, "I Wanna Be Your Man," was released to mixed reviews. It entered the pop charts a week later at number 30 and soon had broken into the Top 20. The Stones did various club dates, recorded what was referred to as an EP (extended-play record) that had four songs on it, and had started writing some songs. Actually, Keith and Mick were writing the songs, pushed hard by Andrew Oldham. His view was that to make themselves even more popular in the long run, they had to start producing and recording their own material rather than that of others. This was new to Keith and Mick, and their first effort ended up being recorded by Gene Pitney, an American pop star. He had made the band's acquaintance in England, backstage at the television show *Thank Your Lucky Stars,* when Pitney was on tour and played the show, as did the Stones. Though a bit bemused by their long hair and seemingly raunchy conduct, Pitney and the band members became fast friends, and he became a big fan of their music. The song he recorded was titled "That Girl Belongs to Yesterday."

Though it was difficult at first, this success with their song inspired Keith and Mick (later referred to as the Glimmer Twins when they began producing the Stones' records) to start spending more time seriously writing songs. Mick did the words and Keith composed the music, which the band would then rearrange as they were presented the new works. This ended up marginalizing Brian, who had been the initial leader of the band. He made some efforts at song writing, but they were either not successful or he wouldn't do them for the band but rather for other acts. Brian's sickliness and his heavier drug use also began to alienate him from his bandmates. He grew more paranoid about his marginalization, which caused him to spend more time alone, thus accelerating the alienation even more. Bill and Charlie, as the backup players, didn't feel the rivalry that Brian, Mick, and Keith had for attention as the front men. It didn't help Brian that he had made side deals with Easton and Oldham so that he would get larger financial shares than the rest of the band. That would come back to haunt him when the rest of the band found out. Eventually, Brian would separate himself enough that the band would push him out, but that was more than five years in the future. At that time, Brian was still working as the contact for large contractual agreements with Andrew Oldham and Eric Easton.

By this time (November 1963), the Beatles had produced their second album and had become as popular in the United States as in the United Kingdom. They were planning their first American tour for February 1964, and American music was beginning to embrace this new sound that reflected, yet modified, American rock and roll.

The Stones were still quite a bit behind the Beatles in recognition and success, but they were having an impact. At the end of the year, the results of a British music magazine poll had the Rolling Stones named as the sixth best British vocal group.

In January 1964, the Rolling Stones went into the Regent Sound Studios to do tracks for what they hoped would be an album. Later in the month they did their second U.K. tour, this time with the American female group the Ronettes, who were the headliners. By the end of the first week, the Stones were topping the bill. The Stones were getting swamped by fans, mostly women, at every venue and at times couldn't make it through the crush of people to get into the venue where they were playing and had to resort to climbing in back windows. The hysterical welcomes were difficult but pleasing to Andrew Loog Oldham, who had actually engineered some of them. The riots that the Stones caused brought great publicity and ultimately greater popularity.

Their popularity was increased through the Stones' third U.K. tour in February, a month when they also were back in the studio, recording three songs with the assistance of Gene Pitney, Phil Spector (the American record producer and impresario), and the Hollies. They also decided to have as their third single "Not Fade Away," a Buddy Holly song, which the group significantly rearranged. Later in the month, three more songs were recorded, including a Jagger-Richards original, "Good Times, Bad Times." By March, "Not Fade Away" had reached number 5 in the British pop charts, and Andrew was working on an American tour for the Stones for sometime in autumn 1964.

The band was now playing as many as six gigs a week and getting well paid for it. They were living in much nicer surroundings and being invited to parties with the most well-known celebrities. In fact, they were themselves now seen as top British celebrities, something that both amused and excited them. Some, like Mick, tried to act nonchalant about this, but it was very important to him and he reveled in it. At a party in early March, Mick met Marianne Faithfull for the first time.

Marianne Faithfull was the daughter of a British military officer who became a university professor and an Austrian mother whose family was part of the Habsburg nobility, though they were left with only a title and no money. Her mother had been a ballerina in her younger years. After her parents were divorced when she was six, Marianne led a sheltered life, most notably as a student in a convent school, though she was not Catholic. She attended the party where she met Jagger with John Dunbar, an art student at Cambridge and her future husband. Faithfull was just 17 at the time. She was beautiful, shy, and exotic. Mick's way of meeting her was to spill a drink down her shirt, which made her initially find him simply boorish. Despite the awkward beginning, Faithfull and Dunbar became friendly with the Stones and attended many parties with them over the next year or two. Dunbar and Faithfull were married in 1965, and she gave birth to a son six months later. Dunbar became a successful artist, but Faithfull became heavily involved with drugs and left her husband in 1966, soon becoming Mick's live-in girlfriend.

Andrew Oldham was also fascinated by Marianne Faithful and, after talking with her, convinced her to do a record demo for him. Keith and Mick wrote a song for her recording session, "As Tears Go By," which became a big hit, reaching number 4 on the pop charts. The Stones later did a version released in 1965.

By this time, in mid-1964, the Stones were playing lots of engagements, but at almost every one the crowds went wild, leading to near-riots. The publicity was great for the band, and Andrew Oldham exploited that both to keep their names in the press and to help raise their fees for appearances. Oldham pushed the idea that Stones fans were so devoted to the group as to almost follow them anywhere. On the release of their first album in April 1964, Oldham said, "The Rolling Stones aren't just a group; they're a way of life." This made parents even more fearful of the group and their potential influence on their children as well as, conversely, making the Stones even more popular with those same young people. The album *The Rolling Stones* with no title or words on the cover shot directly to number 1 in England, stayed there for 12 weeks, and remained in the charts for 67 weeks. The American version was released the next month with the title "England's Newest Hit Makers." It rose to number 11 in the charts in the United States and achieved gold status with more than $1 million in sales. The songs on the album included those from the recording session with Gene Pitney and Phil Spector and included one original song by Keith and Mick, "Tell Me (You're Coming Back to Me)." Two songs were credited to Nanker Phelge, meaning that they were band collaborations. One song, "Not Fade Away," had been released in the United Kingdom but not in the United States, and it appears on the U.S. album and was released as the Stones' third U.S. single, where it had little impact.

The Rolling Stones had now surpassed the Beatles, at least in the United Kingdom, in popularity, and Mick Jagger was voted the most popular singer in England. Everywhere in England the band was mobbed, but they still looked forward to playing in the United States and seeing the reaction there. Eric Easton was working on the scheduling of a U.S. tour, and it finally began in June with the Stones flying to New York City, where about 500 screaming fans met their plane. This pleased and surprised the band since they hadn't thought that they were known as much in the United States.

After two days of press interviews, receptions, and radio/television shows, the band flew to Los Angeles, where their first business was taping Dean Martin's *Hollywood Palace* television show. Martin was a singer, actor, and sometime comedian from the old school; he was 47 years old and liked neither the Stones' music nor their appearance. The Stones were subjected to taunting jokes by Martin, and their best song, "Not Fade Away," was cut from the show when it aired on June 13. The Stones were understandably dejected by this fiasco of an appearance.

Overall the American tour was not a success. The Stones played in San Bernardino; San Antonio; Chicago; Dallas; Minneapolis; Detroit; Omaha; Cleveland; Hershey, Pennsylvania; and New York City, but the crowds were uneven in size, tone, and appreciation. The venues were often large with the crowd small, but those who attended were very enthusiastic. In many of the cities the Stones were mobbed, but in others, like San Antonio, where they appeared at the Fair Grounds, the group was booed by cowboys. Publicity and planning were not well done. One great highlight was the recording sessions, which they had at Chess Records in Chicago, where Muddy Waters, Chuck Berry, and Buddy Guy all dropped by. The sessions went well and the results would be seen when the band released a second album. The biggest problem for the tour was the timing; the Stones did not have a big popular single released in America at the time, and their visit was simply premature. It was a good learning experience so that they would have some idea of what to expect on their next American tour, but there was a great deal of frustration, embarrassment, and exhaustion, which didn't result in the great success that the band had hoped to achieve. Their final two concerts in New York City at Carnegie Hall were huge successes, however, foreshadowing future glory, and the band flew back to London on June 22, 1964.

Oldham scheduled a European tour shortly after the return from the United States, but now the Stones were well known on much of the Continent, and they were harassed by fans everywhere they went. In England, Keith, Mick, and Chrissie Shrimpton moved out and left Andrew to find another place to live, but fans managed to find and break in to the new home of Keith and Mick regularly. Life was becoming much less private as the success of the band continued to rise.[4] Two of the songs recorded at the Chess session in Chicago were released, and "Good Times, Bad Times" became the Stones first number 1 single in Europe, two weeks after its release in late June. Concerts in Ireland, England, and Holland were accompanied by rioting, destructive fans and police escorting the band in and out and, often, hammering on abusive fans.

The rest of the summer and early fall, the Stones continued to tour, while also doing a recording session for another EP, which went to the top of the British charts, and songs for an album, out of which came singles to be released. In late September, "Time Is on My Side" was released in the United States, and "Congratulations" soon followed. The latter was an original of Keith and Mick and reached number 6 in the U.S. charts. A return tour of the United States now seemed most timely, and Eric Easton finally got one scheduled for that fall.

Despite their great popularity and busy schedule, all was not happy within the group. Brian was continuing to ail quite a bit and was often excluded from discussions about the group, and this fueled his justifiable feelings of paranoia. Charlie got married to his long-time girlfriend, Shirley, and Mick was quite angry when he found out. He and Andrew had ordered that Charlie not get married because it would harm the image of the single, "available" Rolling Stones. Bill was mocked by Mick, Keith, and Andrew for marrying and having a child. Brian's five illegitimate children also made him tense and the subject of the group's annoyance at his actions. Finally, the band members were not getting much money. Despite their successes, promoters were not paying them fairly, and the money from recordings was not as large as was to be expected. None of the lads had a lot of money, and this was frustrating them now that they were playing so much and in so many different venues.

In mid-October, the second Stones' album, *12 × 5*, was released in the United States, and about a week later, the band returned to New York City for their second tour. The new album contained mostly songs from the Chicago recording sessions as well as the additional ones done in London. Included were the two singles that had been released in the United States and one other original Richards-Jagger tune, "Grown Up Wrong." The album went to number 3 in the American charts, and that, combined with the success of the singles, made this new tour better timed than the last one.

In New York the Stones had two highly attended concerts at the Academy of Music and also appeared on the leading American television show the *Ed Sullivan Show*. The reception at every venue was largely screaming teenage girls, many breaking down barriers, jumping onto the stage, and attempting to hug or tackle members of the band. Outside the performance venues, it was just as difficult for the Stones. After New York, the band flew to Sacramento for a concert, then on to Los Angeles, where they performed in a film concert called the Teen-Age Music International (T.A.M.I.) Show, along with a host of other well-known acts. These included James Brown, Chuck Berry, the Marvelettes, Gerry and the Pacemakers, and Smokey Robinson and the Miracles. The band also added some great musicians to their own performance: Leon Russell on piano, Nino Tempo on saxophone, and Glen Campbell on guitar. The Stones loved meeting all these musicians and playing with them, and this created lasting friendships among the Stones and these other musicians.

After concerts in San Diego, San Bernardino, and Long Beach, the band flew to Cleveland for a presidential election night concert (Lyndon Johnson was reelected, defeating Barry Goldwater) that was not well attended. Then they went on to Providence, where the Stones were forced to abort the show after five songs because of damage caused by dozens of girls rushing the stage.

Then it was on to New York and Chicago and Chess Studios. The band recorded songs once again, and these would appear on their next album. The band then played a number of medium-sized cities—Milwaukee; Ft. Wayne, Indiana; Louisville; and Dayton, Ohio—before returning to Chicago for their final concert of the tour. The Stones returned to London with the number 1 hit in the United States and the new number 1 hit in England, "Little Red Rooster," a Howlin' Wolf song, recorded in Chicago. The year 1965 was about to begin, and things would only get better and better for the Rolling Stones in this new year.

NOTES

1. Much of this comes from Gomelsky's interview in Mick Jagger, Keith Richards, Charlie Watts, and Ronnie Wood (2003), *According to the Rolling Stones*, ed. Dora Lowenstein and Philip Dodd, London: Weidenfeld and Nicolson, pp. 48–51.

2. Bill Wyman, with Ray Coleman (1990), *Stone Alone: The Story of a Rock 'n Roll Band*, New York: Viking, p. 143.

3. See ibid. This statement of fidelity was made on p. 188 and again on p. 355. In the latter, Wyman and the rest of the Stones count the number of girls that they had been with, and Charlie's total was zero, other than his wife, Shirley.

4. Kris Needs (2004), *Keith Richards: Before They Make Me Run,* London: Plexus, pp. 35, 41.

CHAPTER THREE

The Stones as a Number One Band, 1965–1967

The year 1964 had ended with word that "Little Red Rooster" had been banned from American radio because of sexual connotations. This was somewhat amusing since so many R&B songs had sexual connotations, but the Rolling Stones were now seen as a decadent group of young men, and their products were being scrutinized far more closely. Certainly raising the issue politically made those banning seem like they were protecting the nation's youth. Of course, it only made the Stones and their songs more appealing to that same youthful age group.

In response to the banning, the Stones quickly released another single in the United States in late December, "Heart of Stone." This song would be featured, along with "Little Red Rooster," on the new Stones album *Rolling Stones, Now!* which was released in February 1965 in the United States. The month prior, a British album, *Rolling Stones No. 2,* had been released. The albums were similar but different. The American version had half the songs from the British version and half that would appear on the next British album in the fall. The albums were a mix of blues songs by others like Chuck Berry and three or four originals by Keith and Mick. Besides the five band members, Ian Stewart and Jack Nitzsche played the keyboards on the albums.

In January the band did a tour of Ireland, where they were well received in Belfast, Dublin, and Cork. On their return to London, they barely had time to unpack before setting out on their first tour of Australia and New Zealand. There was a stopover of a couple days in Los Angeles, and the band used some of that time to record five songs, two of which were Mick and Keith songs, "The Last Time" and "Play with Fire"; both would appear on the American version of the new Stones album, which was released the next fall.

The Stones landed in Sydney on January 21, exhausted from the long trip but eager to conquer a new audience and see what they could of Australia. After being met by 3,000 screaming fans at the airport, they realized that seeing the country would be a challenge again, as it was in the United States, but they would see what was possible. They had a floor in a Hilton hotel with a great view of Sydney harbor, so that was a good start. Over two days, the Stones gave five concerts at Agricultural Hall in Sydney to wildly enthusiastic crowds (more than 25,000), though press reviews were predictably negative because of their image as bad boys with long hair.

The band flew to Brisbane, 550 miles north of Sydney, where they gave two sold-out concerts in City Hall. They also got in some water skiing and time in the outback before flying to Melbourne, where they did five shows before more than 20,000 people. The fans were also buying Stones records and the tour was a huge success, despite the generally negative reviews by the local media. That success continued in New Zealand, following a four-hour flight to Christchurch, where the band gave two well-received shows. After less enthusiastic crowds greeted them in the town of Invercargill, the southernmost city in New Zealand, with a population of 50,000, the Stones cut their shows short and rested a bit. Then they flew to Dunedin on the southeast coast of the South Island, where they managed to spend some time touring, visiting a volcanic area and a Maori village. After performing in Dunedin they went on to Auckland and Wellington. The Stones were well received but with nothing like the wild enthusiasm that had characterized most of Australia. Thus they returned to Melbourne and gave two more hastily booked shows, which drew another 10,000 fans.

The band was also finding lots of girls available and took advantage of those opportunities as much as they could. Being that far from England made them bolder than ever in terms of picking up the best-looking girls and spending the night with them. Melbourne, Sydney, and later Adelaide and Perth were all the same in that respect. The band left Australia and arrived in Singapore on February 15, about the time that the album *Rolling Stones, Now!* was released in the United States. It rose to number 5 and stayed on the charts for 52 weeks, the best Stones album to date. After pleasure stopovers in Hong Kong and Los Angeles, once again the Stones were back in London by the end of February.

Another short U.K. tour followed in March with concerts in London, Manchester, Liverpool, Scarborough, and Rugby, among other cities. Accompanying the Stones, who were the headliners, were the Hollies, another young British group. The tour was less than two weeks and culminated with an incident at a service station in East London. Because of the crowds rushing the stage and the hall itself, police usually hurried the Stones out of auditoriums immediately and into waiting cars. Driving away, Bill Wyman needed to use the toilet, and the group stopped at a service station, but the attendant claimed that there was no working toilet. After arguing with the attendant, three of the Stones (Mick, Brian, and Bill) walked down the road a bit and urinated on the wall. They left but were later charged with "insulting behavior" and tried in a magistrate's court three months later. They were found guilty and fined five pounds each. This would have hardly been news, except that it was the Rolling Stones, and it seemed to show how rude, uncouth, and dangerous they were, so claimed some members of the media.

In late March the group did a Nordic tour beginning in Copenhagen, where they played to 4,000, then on to Stockholm and Gothenburg, where the boys had great concerts, two of them at Tivoli Gardens in the center of Copenhagen. A week or two later the band was back on the road, this time to Paris for three shows on Easter weekend, all of which were sold out. Three days after returning to London, the band was off for their first tour of Canada, starting in Montreal on April 23. They then drove to Ottawa for a second concert, and on to Toronto and London, Ontario. There were problems at all of the venues; the noise and out-of-control crowd in Toronto caused the Stones to abbreviate their performance, and in London the police turned off the power and a small riot ensued. The Stones were seen as the problem, though their fans, now showing up in force, were simply uncontrollable at times.

From Canada the Stones flew to New York to start their third American tour in late April 1965. They were invited back to the *Ed Sullivan Show* and rehearsed at the studio for that appearance, but their first live gig was to be in Albany, 150 miles north of

The Rolling Stones arrive in Montreal, Canada, in April 1965: top left, Mick Jagger; top right, Charlie Watts; middle left, Keith Richards; middle right, Brian Jones; bottom, Bill Wyman. (AP-650422057)

New York City. There they did two shows before 2,000 fans at each show, with the police tightly guarding the stage and the dressing rooms. The band returned to New York City where they did an afternoon show at the Academy of Music on Saturday, May 1, then were driven to Philadelphia, 80 miles south, where they did an evening show at Convention Hall, hosted by Dick Clark of the television show *American Bandstand,* with 13,000 fans in attendance.

The Stones returned to New York to do the *Ed Sullivan Show* the next night, where they performed four songs and received excellent reviews in the media. The band was being praised for their music rather than criticized for their hair or their clothing. Though there was still great disagreement, more and more people, not just teens, were beginning to accept the Stones as a legitimate band and thrill to their music.

Though the band loved the reception, they were having their own problems. Brian's paranoia, his increased use of alcohol and drugs (particularly LSD), and his callous treatment of the girls he picked up were becoming more bothersome to the other band members and their road crew. When Brian beat up a young groupie who he'd picked up, he was taken to task by the other band members and was even beaten up himself in retaliation by one of the crew. Mick and Keith were using more and more marijuana, as was Bill. Charlie seemed to be uninterested in it.[1]

From New York, the band went on to concerts in Statesboro, Georgia, and Clearwater, Florida, the latter at a baseball stadium with 4,000 fans, who were screaming, stomping, and pelting the field with debris in anticipation of the Stones' arrival. The police issued warnings about canceling the show if the unruliness continued, but it was ignored as the Stones began playing. Hordes of teens rushed the police and taunted them, and they responded by aborting the concert after four songs. Though such incidents were not their fault, the Stones were gaining a reputation for the riots that they seemed to cause, and they were getting tired of their attenuated concerts.

Many localities decided to ban further rock concerts following the appearance of the Stones or the Beatles (or even before that). The police were not accustomed to such behavior, and local governments decided that the cost (or profit) was not worth the time and trouble involved with these appearances. Young fans were just responding as they had since the bobby-soxers of the 1940s had swooned over the likes of Frank Sinatra. The teens were just becoming more persistent in the pursuit of their idols.

The next concert, in Birmingham, Alabama, was at Legion Field before 20,000 fans, and a number of other acts, such as the Beach Boys and the Righteous Brothers, also performed. There were no incidents, and the Stones went on to Jacksonville, Florida, before going on May 9 to Chicago, a city where they enjoyed visiting and recording music.

The next day, they spent nine hours at Chess Studios recording, including "Satisfaction," a song that Keith had heard in a dream a week or so before while sleeping in their motel in Clearwater. He had gotten up and recorded the distinctive chords that characterize "Satisfaction" at his bedside then gone back to bed. The next day he played the chords for the band, and Mick came up with words. Both of them thought it might be a nice little number but not worth really recording. The other band members disagreed, and over the initial objections of Keith and Mick, the song was recorded for release.[2]

The next day the Stones flew to Los Angeles for recording sessions on May 12 and 13, both of which went well into the night. There they perfected "Satisfaction," utilizing the fuzz box, an effects pedal that distorts sound. The band and the sound engineers decided that this song would be their next single release, and it became their first number 1 hit in the United States when it was released in early June 1965.

After the two studio days, the band flew to San Francisco for a gig before 5,000. Following that, they were in San Bernardino (the scene of their first big successful concert in the United States, on their first tour), Long Beach, San Diego, Fresno, San Jose, and Sacramento. The band appeared in Los Angeles on the television show *Shindig*, where they premiered "Satisfaction" on May 20. The band also demanded that Howlin' Wolf and Son House be on the show, and they were. Both of the old bluesmen were over 55 at this point, but the Stones were enthralled by their abilities and were honored to have them on the show. After the California tour, the Stones returned to New York City for three shows before flying back to London; they had been gone over a month.

The band members were all exhausted and attempted to vacation quietly before beginning another tour of Scotland in mid-June and their second tour of Scandinavia at the end of that month. In most of the concerts, at this point, the Stones could not be heard over the unending screams of the teenage girls in the audience. They were seen, of course, and many of the fans still made efforts to touch, grab, or rip at their clothing, but the increased police security made this increasingly difficult. Oslo, Norway; Copenhagen, Denmark; Malmo, Sweden; and Yyteri Beach (near Pori), Finland were the venues for the concerts on this tour.

Despite these huge successes, the band members did not have a lot of money, and they were perplexed and angry that the money generated seemed to be disappearing. Andrew Oldham, never a great one at accounting, decided that he'd find someone else to handle this aspect of the Stones and approached an American accountant named Allen Klein, who had managed to "collect" (as clients) the Dave Clark Five, the Animals, Donovan, and Herman's Hermits as well as a large stable of American performers, in July 1965. The idea was that he must be good, so the Stones would greatly benefit by having him as their exclusive representative and business manager. Oldham, by this time, was heavily involved with drugs, including amphetamines, barbiturates, and LSD, and was showing signs of manic depression; he willingly signed away major rights to the Stones without really knowing what he was doing. He returned to London about 10 days later and met with Mick and Keith to sell them on Klein. Then the whole group met to discuss the deal and decided to agree, though Bill Wyman had great reservations. He was shouted down by the group.[3]

Initially, Klein and Oldham seemed to be able to deliver, especially in a much better contract with Decca, the Stones' recording company. They each received big up-front checks and guarantees of payments for the next 10 years. The money assuaged all fears, temporarily.

After this, the Stones returned to touring England with 13 shows over the next month; then, after 10 days, an exhausting tour of Ireland, Germany, Austria, Scotland, and once again England ensued. They did 61 shows in 75 days and were wearing down. Mick and Chrissie Shrimpton attended parties with royalty, including Princess Margaret, the queen's younger sister. She and Mick became very close, and he later built a home on the secluded West Indian island of Mustique, adjacent to her villa.

During the first U.K. tour in July, the album *Out of Our Heads* was released in the United States. A slightly different version would be released in September in England. The album was the result of the recording sessions in Chicago at Chess and Los Angeles at RCA. The album would be the first Stones LP to hit number 1 in the United States, and it stayed in the charts for over a year. This would also be one of the last albums to include many songs written by others besides the Stones. There were six such songs, with four by Keith and Mick, including "Satisfaction" and "The Last Time." Two songs were credited to Nanker Phelge, meaning that they were band collaborations. This included "Play with Fire."

The next big tour began September 3 with two shows in Dublin, the second of which ended in a riot, with instruments being smashed and band members knocked around as audience members assaulted the stage. The band encouraged audience members to get excited, but a likely combination of alcohol and hooliganism got the audience completely out of control. Bill Wyman suffered a sprained arm, but the group managed to escape to a waiting car and went on to Belfast for the next two shows. After those, the band flew to London, then on to Los Angeles for a recording session, which went through the night. The band was jet-lagged and overworked, and the tour hadn't really started yet. They returned to London, slept a bit, then flew to the Isle of Man, in the Irish Sea, for a show on September 8.

The Stones flew to Germany for the continuation of the tour and to meet a person who would change the dynamic of the group significantly. This was Anita Pallenberg, a 21-year-old model who attended the show in Munich on September 14 then somehow got backstage between shows and made the acquaintance of Mick, followed by Brian and Keith. This was the fourth stop in Germany after packed double shows in Munster, Essen, and Hamburg. Pallenberg was in Munich for a modeling assignment and managed to get a Swedish photographer to smuggle her backstage. Her mother was German and her father was Italian, and she was fluent in at least four languages. She noticed Brian Jones and she came up to talk to him but saw that he was near tears. Brian had just been lambasted by the other band members for his callous treatment of Pat Andrews, the mother of one of his children, whom he continued to lead on then reject cruelly. Brian told Anita that he needed her and she returned to the hotel with him after the show and spent the night. This was the beginning of Anita's role as Brian's girlfriend, which would end painfully (for Brian) within two years.

As for the other Stones, the tour next went to Berlin and Vienna before returning to London for a week of rest. In Berlin Mick paraded around the stage, goose-stepping in a way reminiscent of the Nazis of World War II and sending an unruly crowd into more disarray. The fans were so wild initially that the Stones had to retreat to their dressing room after just one number because of the fans who had rushed the stage and started attacking the Stones. When order was restored, they returned, but rioting continued on stage and in the stands, and more than 60 fans were taken to the hospital with various injuries. At the end of the concert, the Stones ran from the stage to their dressing room, which was in old World War II bunkers, then followed tunnels out to waiting cars and back to the hotel. In Vienna, there were bomb threats, and over 800 police were present for security, but the crowd stayed under control. The Stones did rather foment outrageousness, but the seemingly total anarchy that was loosed on them was much more than they had bargained for, again likely fueled by alcohol and increasing rebelliousness among many young people in society.

On the return to London, Anita Pallenberg followed and moved in with Brian Jones. The band had a week off before beginning their sixth tour of England and Scotland, which would run just over three weeks and encompass 48 shows, 2 per day. It was a hellish pace and was bound to be accompanied by the Stones seeking whatever recreation they could find in their few off hours, whether it was drugs, alcohol, or women. The tour was done along with the Spencer Davis group, whose lead singer at times was 17-year-old Stevie Winwood. Other groups sat in, such as the Moody Blues, but these appearances were sporadic. The tour coincided with the release of the Stones' newest single, "Get Off of My Cloud," in the United States, where it became their sixth gold record and rose to number 2 in the charts. A month later it was released in England and rose to number 1, where it remained for three weeks.

Not only was the tour successful but other outside factors indicated the growing international respect for the Stones and their musical abilities. Three of their songs were covered by other artists, as diverse as Otis Redding, Quincy Jones, and an English dance band. Bill had formed his own musical company and was producing other acts, and Mick and Keith had also formed a separate music production company. The Beatles had been recognized by the queen with awards of MBE entering them into the Order of the British Empire. The Stones were seen as the alternative, a rather antiestablishment order, awarded by the youth of the nation (and other nations). Though there was really little difference personally in the characters of the Beatles and the Stones, the media created a rivalry that didn't really exist but one that was exploited for publicity purposes. In reality, the members of the groups were good friends; they simply had slightly different approaches to music writing and production.

After the two sold-out shows in London's Granada Theatre on October 17, the Stones again had a short break before returning to North America once again for a six-week tour of Canada and the United States. On arrival in Manhattan on October 27, 1965, the Stones were amazed to see a 100-foot-high billboard of their picture overlooking Times Square, part of the promotion for their new album *December's Children*, which would come out during the American tour. The promo was the work of their new manager, Allen Klein, and it provided some confidence (ill placed, as it turned out) that they would be well served by Klein. The album liner notes were again by Andrew Oldham and seen as mysterious and enigmatic by some but were actually drug-induced and nonsensical, as noted by others.[4]

The tour was to be conducted via chartered private plane with a number of other accompanying acts. Having the plane would eliminate the crush of fans at commercial airports and allow the band to come and go at their schedule, not that of the airlines. The first stop was Montreal on October 29 at the Forum (where the Montreal Canadiens hockey team played), and there, 8,000 fans went crazy and many stormed the stage, overwhelming security and destroying Charlie's drum kit. The band was happy to escape to their plane and fly on to concerts in Ithaca, New York (Cornell University) in the afternoon and Syracuse's War Memorial Auditorium in the evening. These shows were peacefully received, and the band then flew to Toronto for a show the next night in Maple Leaf Gardens (another hockey venue). Unlike six months before, the security controlled the 13,000 fans, and the concert was a great success, with the Stones (especially Brian) beginning to use new instruments in concert. Brian's use of the electric organ on "Play with Fire," which had not even included him at all in the original recording, was an exciting touch.

In Rochester the next day, the police security failed and the concert was stopped after six songs. Concerts in Rhode Island, Connecticut, and Boston (at the Boston Garden, a basketball and hockey venue) went off well. On November 6 the Stones gave an afternoon concert in Manhattan, then an evening concert in Philadelphia's Convention Hall, as they had done on their last American tour. They returned to New York after the show and met Bob Dylan, who took Brian Jones on a tour of Greenwich Village clubs. Then there were two shows in Newark, just across the river in New Jersey, before a couple days off, spent in New York, where a massive power outage caused the Stones to be trapped in their hotel because the elevators weren't working. They had an all-night party that included Bob Dylan, Robbie Robertson, and others and involved drugs, sex, and wild music making.

The band flew to North Carolina for concerts in Raleigh and Greensboro, then appeared in Washington at the Coliseum for a show on Saturday afternoon, followed by one that evening in Baltimore. Over the next week, there would be shows in Knoxville, Tennessee; Charlotte; Nashville; Memphis; and Shreveport, Louisiana. Then, on November 21, the Stones did two shows: an afternoon performance in Fort Worth and an evening one in Dallas. For most of these shows the band was getting $15,000 (median annual income in the United States at that time was just under $8,000), and they finally envisioned getting rich from their music, though legal problems with Allen Klein would make this more difficult. There was a three-day break after Memphis and before Shreveport, and the band went to Miami to relax. Anita Pallenberg flew in to be with Brian.

From Texas the band went on to Tulsa, Pittsburgh, Milwaukee, and Detroit before doing two shows on Saturday (November 27) in Dayton and Cincinnati, followed by two shows on Sunday in Chicago's Arie Crown Theatre. This tour allowed no down time in Chicago, and they did a show in Denver the next day; Phoenix on Tuesday; Vancouver on Wednesday; Seattle on Thursday; Sacramento on Friday; two shows in San Jose on Saturday; and two more in Los Angeles at the Sports Arena on Sunday, December 5. This ended the exhausting tour and the band's touring for the remainder of 1965. The end of the tour coincided with the release of *December's Children*, which rose to number 4 in the United States and remained in the charts for 34 weeks. Chrissie Shrimpton flew out to join Mick for the end-of-tour party in Los Angeles and accompany him back to London. Mick, who had been spending many nights on the tour with Patti LaBelle, immediately avoided her, and their relationship cooled swiftly. Anita Pallenberg had joined the tour at some point, and she and Brian often used LSD, which fed Brian's paranoia and made him unreliable on stage. The other Stones were angry about his lack of performance and let him know it. This only made his other mental problems worse. Anita's encouragement in his drug use (and hers) exacerbated a bad situation.

Before leaving California, the Stones went once again to RCA Studios for a three-day recording session at a facility and recording crew with whom they felt very confident. During these sessions they recorded 10 songs, some of which would constitute the next album, *Aftermath*, which would be released in spring 1966. In the sessions Charlie experimented with playing a number of different percussion instruments, including bongos, timpani, and congas, while Brian experimented with a harpsichord and extended his harmonica abilities on a few songs.

The end-of-year polling in England had the Stones as the top group (second was the Beatles) and "Satisfaction" as the top song. In the United States the Beatles still held the position as top group, but the Rolling Stones were close behind. "Satisfaction" was also the top single in the United States that year. The Stones had six gold records in the year, and the Beatles eight. Groups like Herman's Hermits, the Hollies, the Animals, Gerry and the Pacemakers, and the Dave Clark Five showed the surprisingly swift rise of British groups in the United States.

The Stones took a few weeks off before heading on the road again in February. They were headed to Australia and went via North

America, first landing in New York, where they appeared once again on the *Ed Sullivan Show*, this time in their first color broadcast. They rehearsed, then did three numbers live: "Satisfaction," "As Tears Go By" (the song written originally for Marianne Faithfull), and "19th Nervous Breakdown," their latest single, released a week before and which rose to number 2 on the charts.

From New York the band flew to Los Angeles, then Hawaii and Fiji, before arriving in Sydney on February 16. Transoceanic travel required more stopovers because of the limited fuel capacities of the airplanes at that time. The tour would go two weeks, and the Stones would do 20 shows, their usual exhausting itinerary but limited to bigger cities and venues, especially in New Zealand. The band did five shows in Sydney before more than 25,000 fans. Each performance was preceded by the opening band for the tour, the Searchers, a British band.

After an off day, the tour went to Brisbane for two shows, then on to Adelaide for one performance. Over the following four days the Stones did eight shows in Melbourne, where they had been so popular on their last tour. This time the press reviews matched the acclaim of the fans. The Stones were no longer being put down for their appearance and were being lauded for their musical expertise and stage presence. Shows then followed in Wellington and Auckland, New Zealand, before the band flew to Perth in Western Australia for the final show of the tour.

The trip home again went through Los Angeles and again involved a recording session at RCA Studios. In four days they recorded over 20 songs, and the band saw it as their most fruitful and creative session ever. All the songs were by Keith and Mick, but the variety of instrumentation that Brian exhibited was a key to the greatness of a number of the songs. The band members left Los Angeles on March 12; some flew to London, while Brian and Andrew Oldham traveled to New York for a few days. On returning to London, both Keith and Bill were frustrated in efforts to gain access to their own funds, frozen in New York banks by Allen Klein. Financially, things were as bad as ever and looked to be getting worse as the Stones, supposed millionaires, could not get their own money.

The resolution of their financial questions would take years to resolve, and the Stones would be busy during all that time performing and recording. After two weeks of rest the Stones were off on another 10-day tour, this time of Western Europe. They played seven shows in six days in Belgium, Holland, and France. Two shows in Stockholm and two in Copenhagen followed, completing the tour on April 5. At the end of this tour a Rolling Stones compilation album titled *Big Hits, High Tides, and Green Grass* was released in the United States. It included songs mostly from the previous two albums, went to number 3 in the charts, and remained listed for almost two years, earning multiplatinum status. (The U.K. version was released in November and remained in the charts for 43 weeks.)

Ten days after the latest tour ended, *Aftermath* was released in the United Kingdom. This was the first album with all Jagger-Richards songs and was the result of the recording sessions at RCA Studios in Los Angeles. The album was an immediate hit, reaching number 1 in the United Kingdom, with the American version (released in late June) going to number 2. The variety of music and instruments on the album continues to make this one of the finest albums the Stones ever did and one of the best rock albums ever. Three singles from the album, "Paint It Black," "Mother's Little Helper," and "Lady Jane," ended up the year as numbers 1, 8, and 24, respectively, on the American charts for the year 1966. On "Paint It Black," the melody is carried by the haunting sound of a sitar, played by Brian Jones, self-taught with the guidance of George Harrison. On "Lady Jane," Jones captures the tone of the song through his dulcimer playing. The song had many stories about who or what it was directed toward, including a wife of Henry VIII (Jane Seymour), Chrissie Shrimpton, and Lady Jane Ormsby-Gore, but one writer says conclusively that the inspiration for Mick was from D. H. Lawrence, a favorite author. In that novel, the gamekeeper protagonist refers to his lover's female parts as Lady Jane. In another song, "Under My Thumb," Brian Jones carries the song with his playing of the marimbas. The last song on the album, "Goin' Home," was a long jam session, initially meant to be a two to three minute song that just went on.

In June the stress of being Mick Jagger finally caught up to him, and he suffered a nervous breakdown.[5] The travel, the recording until all hours, the songwriting with Keith in free time, as well as the partying, were obviously wearing, but the relationship with Chrissie Shrimpton, which combined angry fights with passionate lovemaking, was probably the biggest factor. This would lead to an acrimonious but necessary breakup of the two.

Meanwhile, Marianne Faithfull and her husband, John Dunbar, were also going through a breakup. Faithfull took her son and left in midsummer for Positano, Italy. She returned but left the marriage for good in October. She had a successful pop music career and was now heavily into marijuana use, on a daily basis. She would go on to dangerous drugs within months. Her husband was even more involved with drugs than she and was not making enough money for her to live the way she wanted to. She had gotten close to the Stones, having had brief affairs with Brian, then Keith, and then Mick. That latter relationship would soon begin to grow.

Mick recovered after two weeks of relative isolation, and the band began another North American tour (32 shows in 35 days) on June 24 in Lynn, Massachusetts. With the great success of the *Aftermath* album and the number 1 single "Paint It Black," hopes were high for a very profitable tour. The Manning Bowl in Lynn had 15,000 in attendance. Security was adequate until the final number, when hordes broke through the barriers and the police responded with tear gas. The Stones fled to two waiting vehicles. The next day, Saturday, the group played at Cleveland in the afternoon and Pittsburgh in the evening, and the following day they did an afternoon performance in Washington, D.C., and an evening one in Baltimore. Then followed Hartford, Buffalo, Toronto, Montreal, and Atlantic City, before an appearance in the Tennis Stadium at Forest Hills, Queens, New York, before 9,400 fans in a stadium seating 12,000. (The more expensive seats went unsold.) This followed a press conference at the West 79th Street Marina, held to celebrate the release of both *Aftermath* in the United States and the singles "Mother's Little Helper" and "Lady Jane," done on the same day. The Stones helicoptered in and out, timely, indeed, after the fans rushed the stage once again.

From New York the toured wended through New Jersey, Virginia, Michigan, Indiana, Illinois (only a brief stop in Chicago this time), Texas, Missouri, Nebraska, Manitoba, and British Columbia in Canada, Washington, Oregon, and into California in late July. First was a show in Sacramento, then on July 25, more than 17,000 fans filed into the Hollywood Bowl for the sold-out concert. The next day was Mick's 23rd birthday and the last mainland performance in San Francisco. A show two days later in Honolulu ended the tour and also gave the band time to relax after the tour. Then they returned to Los Angeles for a couple more weeks of recovery. Bill's wife, Diane; Charlie's wife, Shirley; and Chrissie Shrimpton joined the entourage in Los Angeles for the holiday. The band returned to London until September 11, when they flew to New York for another taping of the *Ed Sullivan Show*. This time they lip-synched to "Paint It Black," "Lady Jane," and "Have You Seen Your Mother Baby?" because Brian had a broken wrist, the result of a fight that he had had with Anita Pallenberg while they vacationed in Morocco.

Ten days later the Stones began a 17-day tour of the United Kingdom, accompanied by Ike and Tina Turner and the Yardbirds. Playing mostly two shows a day, the tour did 16 shows in 10 days, then 8 more in 4 days, after a 4-day break in the middle of the tour, ending in Southampton on October 9, 1966. The Stones would not tour again for six months.

During the subsequent six months, a number of significant events would occur. Marianne Faithfull left her husband and started an affair with Mick Jagger. It remained clandestine for weeks while Mick tried to figure out how to end his relationship with Chrissie Shrimpton. That did not occur until mid-December. In November the Stones went back into the recording studio in London and finished what they had started in Los Angeles in August, that is, the next album, which would be released in the United Kingdom in January 1967. In December the Stones' first live album, *Got Live If You Want It*, with music seemingly drawn from concerts on October 1 and 7 in Newcastle-upon-Tyne and Bristol, respectively, was released in the United States. The quality was not great, and the Stones subsequently disowned the album, despite the fact that it went gold. The year ended with the Stones having two million-selling albums and four singles that sold a million copies. The three biggest record sellers were the Stones, the Beatles and Elvis Presley. There was no question that the Rolling Stones were one of the top musical acts in the world, and they commanded the respect of critics for their song composition and performance.

NOTES

1. Bill Wyman, with Ray Coleman (1990), *Stone Alone: The Story of a Rock 'n Roll Band*, New York: Viking, pp. 315–16. On marijuana smoking, then, see ibid., p. 322, and Alan Clayson (2003), *Brian Jones*, London: Sanctuary, p. 138.
2. Wyman, *Stone Alone*, p. 316; Stephen Davis (2001), *Old Gods Almost Dead: The 40-Year Odyssey of the Rolling Stones*, New York: Broadway Books, p. 122.
3. See Davis, *Old Gods Almost Dead*, pp. 131–32; Wyman, *Stone Alone*, p. 329; Christopher Andersen (1993), *Jagger, Unauthorized*, New York: Delacorte Press, p. 117.
4. See Andersen, *Jagger, Unauthorized*, p. 119.
5. See Wyman, *Stone Alone*, pp. 378–79; Andersen, *Jagger, Unauthorized*, p. 124.

CHAPTER FOUR

Battles with the Beatles, Drugs, and the Establishment

The year 1967 marked a time when many of the social forces that had been growing in the United States came to flower and had effects on England, the European continent, and beyond. The American civil rights movement had begun to gain more attention in the mid-1950s, and this would have great impact on the segregation and unequal justice seen in much of the United States, most notably in the American South. The roots of blues music were direct derivatives of the songs sung by African slaves and their descendants in the South. Slavery was abolished in the British West Indies in 1833 and had not been allowed in England since it was abolished by common law in the 1300s. The Rolling Stones' only contact with African Americans was through the music of rhythm and blues, so it was not until the Stones first toured the United States that they actually saw the harsh realities of segregation and its aftereffects. They were significantly affected by this and became outspoken in their disgust with segregation, yet they saw little that they could do to alter the social situation in the United States.

American armed forces had been present in South Vietnam since the French had abandoned the country after their defeat by the Viet Minh Communist forces in 1954. What began as an advisory role had escalated by 1967 to a large-scale American ground war, and this caused great dissension in American society. The antiwar movement was brought together with the civil rights movement, in the middle to late 1960s, by notables like Dr. Martin Luther King Jr. This was because the war was being fought largely by troops who were poor and minority members. As the resistance to the war grew, many musicians were outspoken in their support of the antiwar movement. The Stones, most notably Mick Jagger, were among those music group members who spoke out for peace and ending war. The Stones, however, were never greatly involved in antiwar protests, as John Lennon of the Beatles was.

The 1950s had been a period of relative calm though very unsettling because of cold war tensions between the Soviet Union and the Western powers of Europe and the United States. The civil rights movement gave voice to the free speech movement in colleges and universities, which gave rise to antiwar protesters and the questioning of authority by many in the so-called baby boom generation. Along with that came a change in music and musical tastes. The swing music and ballads of the 1940s began to be challenged by rhythm and blues, more noticeable once white musicians adapted the genre that had been created by blacks. To the Rolling Stones, it was the sound that was intriguing, not whether it was made by black or white musicians, and they set out to imitate (and later create) their versions of such musical sounds. By 1967, rhythm and blues had also created the notion of rock and roll music, which kept reshaping itself.

The Stones' music during this period reflects this continual growth and reshaping of the musical form. This can be seen in the changes in their albums from *December's Children* in 1965 to *Aftermath* in 1966 to *Between the Buttons* in 1967. This latter album was the result of studio work in Los Angeles and London in late 1966. The influence of Andrew Oldham's mentor, Phil Spector, is obvious in a number of the album's cuts that feature layered music (which was referred to in Spector's case as a wall of sound). "My Obsession," "Yesterday's Papers," and "Complicated" are the three most notable examples. The second song was likely about Jagger's breakup with Chrissie Shrimpton and the latter song about his new girl, Marianne Faithfull. The most controversial song on the U.S. album was "Let's Spend the Night Together," simply because of the blatant invitation of the title. It was this song (of the three sung) that was censored by Ed Sullivan when the Stones flew back to New York to appear in January 1967. Sullivan told the band that he would not allow those lyrics to be sung on his show, and they reluctantly agreed to his demand to alter the words to "let's spend some time together." At least three different times, when those lyrics were sung live on the show, Mick rolled his eyes to indicate his disgust with the altered lyrics, and Bill Wyman did so once, when the cameras were on him. This appearance, for which the Stones flew to New York and then back to London, was another indication of their enormous popularity.

Besides this appearance and a couple for British television, the Stones were mostly caught up in personal adventures during the early part of the year. Mick had dumped Chrissie Shrimpton and was living with Marianne Faithfull in a different house outside London. Bill was separated from his wife, Diane, and was beginning a long relationship with Astrid Lundstrom. Brian and Anita Pallenberg were still together, but his abusive treatment finally resulted in her leaving him and moving in with Keith, with whom she would live for the next 10 years. The most notable incident of this period occurred in February, when Keith had a small party for a few friends at his new home, Redlands. Following a London recording session on Saturday, February 11, a group of nine, including Keith, Mick, and Marianne, drove to Keith's new home outside London. Earlier in February, the British newspaper *News of the World* had written a story describing in detail Mick's use of LSD at a party hosted by another British band, the Moody Blues. The story was completely erroneous since the actual person involved was Brian Jones. Mick brought suit against the paper for defamation, after which he was put under surveillance by someone, likely an informant, working for the *News of the World*. On February 11, the police received a call informing them that there were drugs being consumed at a party at Redlands, and they subsequently came to the home Sunday night with a search warrant.

Depending on whose version one accepts, the partygoers were using marijuana, after having taken an LSD trip earlier in the day, when the police arrived unexpectedly, and Marianne, having just bathed, was lounging in the living room wrapped in a bearskin rug and nothing else. Illegal pills were found in Mick's jacket upstairs that were Marianne's but claimed by Mick to protect her. Heroin was found on another guest. The LSD supplier, a young Canadian or American, managed to leave the home with most of his drug wares since they were in foil packets in a briefcase that he convinced the police held exposed film that would be ruined if they opened the case. This mysterious person managed to slip out of the country without being delayed by customs officials. Retrospective consensus among the participants is that this individual was a paid informant. Keith

Brian Jones and Anita Pallenberg at Heathrow Airport, London, September 13, 1967; they illustrate the mod clothing of the period. (AP-6709130238)

Richards was held accountable for all drugs found on the premises that were not claimed by someone else.

The subsequent arrests of Richards and Jagger fed the dissolute reputation of the Stones. Later the Stones tried to use the suggestion of an advisor, who supplied drugs to Keith. He said that he thought that the Stones could get the charges dropped by providing about $12,000 in bribe money through the dealer, "Spanish Tony" Sanchez, which he delivered. Though it seemed to quiet things, his contention that the charges would be dropped was not true, and a hearing was set for May. However, before that, the Stones went about as if there were no charges. They finished the recording sessions in London, some of which would be on the *Flowers* album, released only in the United States in June, and had mostly numbers from some previous releases and other songs that would appear on *Their Satanic Majesties Request*, released in December.

In March Mick and Marianne flew to Morocco for a vacation and were to be joined by, among others, Brian, Anita, and Keith, who were being driven there in Keith's chauffeur-driven Bentley.

Brian got a severe asthma attack in France and was hospitalized but urged Anita and Keith to continue to Morocco, where he hoped to join them. Left alone, the two almost immediately made love in the car then continued in Morocco, ultimately becoming a couple and further adding to Brian's paranoia and depression. When he arrived in Morocco, he sensed that there was something going on, and this led to many arguments and physical fights. Near the end of the time in Morocco, Brian brought two prostitutes to the villa and insisted that Anita engage with him and them. She refused, Brian beat her up, and the next day she and Keith flew back to London. When he returned to London, Brian tried to reconcile, but Anita refused, and that was the worst blow to what was left of Brian's fragile and drug-addled ego.

Nevertheless, shortly afterward, beginning on March 25, the Stones set off on a three week European tour, with 25 shows in 23 days. Beginning in Malmo, then Orebro, Sweden, the Stones gave strong concerts to raucous crowds, where riots were narrowly avoided. There were then concerts in Bremen, Cologne, Dortmund, and Hamburg in Germany, with little incident. In Vienna, however, there was again rioting, when the Stones did two shows, each with 14,000 fans, at the Stadhalle. After a couple days off, the tour continued in Italy with shows in Bologna, Milan, Rome, and Genoa before two big shows in Paris on April 11.

Then the Stones did a concert in a most unlikely country, Poland, still firmly in the grip of the Soviet Union. This was not done for money but rather because the Stones had heard that they had many fans in the Eastern Bloc and wanted to show their goodwill toward them. The Stones witnessed repression and shortages, and many of their most loyal fans weren't able to attend the concert since top government connections seemed to be necessary to occupy many of the seats. They did drive around Warsaw with their guide, distributing free records to fans protesting on the street against being excluded from the concert. This made them feel a bit better, and the next day they flew to Zurich, where Mick was assaulted by a fan on stage, and 12,000 fans rioted; then they flew to The Hague in Holland and finally to Athens, where the tour ended. The Beatles had retired from the road and the Stones would not tour again for more than two years. Their "last" tour, however, finally brought them into American mainstream consciousness with an article focusing on them in *Time* magazine. With no real music magazines (*Rolling Stone* was a broadsheet newspaper which began publishing that year), this coverage was a testimony to the real arrival of the Stones in American music and culture.

In May the Stones' hearing yielded pleas of not guilty and led to a trial date set for June. Shortly after the hearing the police raided Brian Jones's home, confiscated drugs, and charged him with use and possession. The police were after the Rolling Stones.

It was at this time that the personal friendships between the Stones and the Beatles became even stronger. The Beatles began recording *Sgt. Pepper's Lonely Hearts Club Band* in December and released the precedent-setting album in June 1967. This was a so-called concept album and took months to actually record, mix, and refine. A bit of homage to the Stones was paid in the form of the cover photo of the album. The Stones returned the favor in depicting the Beatles on the cover of their next album, also a concept album, *Their Satanic Majesties Request.* Both Lennon and McCartney sang backup vocals on this album, but it was not nearly as well received as *Sgt. Pepper.* The album was seen as an attempt to imitate and outdo the Beatles, and a poor attempt at that. There is a mixture of electronic, psychedelic music and the use of other kinds of music and instruments. This was the state of rock music at that time and was heavily influenced by the drug usage of many of the musicians. The album was recorded between February and October 1967 and released in December in both the United States and the United Kingdom as the same album. It was also the first and only album produced by the Stones themselves.

Andrew Oldham, lost in a drug-induced world, was undergoing electroshock therapy, and the band simply ignored his suggestions on the album until he walked out. That ended the relationship between him and the Stones, leaving their dealings solely in the hands of Allen Klein, where they were confusing and probably fraudulent.[1] The Stones were too busy to keep track of the business dealings, but they did know that they were not receiving what they should be. Klein had their money and doled it out to them only after specific requests were made. The Stones seemed powerless to figure out how to alter that situation. In one sense, Klein's caution probably kept the Stones from blowing much of their money on needless items, but Klein also used the band's money to further his own enterprises and intertwined their money with his fees. It would take years to unwind all that.

In June the Redlands case came to trial, and both Keith and Mick were initially convicted of possession of dangerous drugs, although the drugs in question were not the same. Keith received a fine and a year in jail, Mick a fine and three months' incarceration. They were briefly imprisoned before being granted bail while their cases were appealed. They were also required to turn in their passports since they were not to leave England. All of this caused tremendous fear and stress in Brian Jones, whose trial for his recent drug bust was coming up. His depression spiraled and he was at times completely morose. On July 5 he was admitted to a psychiatric clinic, where he remained for treatment until July 24. Though he seemed better, Brian was never the same again, and he continued to struggle through life.

On July 31 an appeals court threw out Richards's conviction and reduced Jagger's to a year of probation. This may have been a response, in part, to the tremendous outpouring of sympathy and anger over the convictions. The Stones were finally embraced, in this unusual way, by the establishment as well as the youth of the nation and beyond. Even *The Times* of London, the most respected and established newspaper in England, had come out in an editorial for a severe reduction in the sentences. Despite the drug convictions, the Stones, like most rock musicians of the time, continued their drug use, just with more discretion. Jagger in particular confined most of his drug use to home, with Marianne, though he did attend parties with British lords and ladies where drug use was prevalent. London in the late 1960s was the center of style, fashion, music, and other avant-garde events, and drugs were an integral part of much of that.

A stunning coda to this was Brian being convicted of marijuana possession in October and being sentenced to six months in the dreaded Wormwood Prison. He spent a horrid night there before being released on bail as his case was appealed. At about that same time, John Lennon, Paul McCartney, Mick Jagger, and Keith Richards discussed having the two groups (the Beatles and the Rolling Stones) form their own record production organization. These discussions were very preliminary and ended with a news release on October 17 denying that such a merger would take place. Still the two groups remained close in many ways. Two weeks later, Brian Jones received a sentence of nine months in prison for allowing cannabis (marijuana) to be consumed in his home. Immediately, that decision was appealed.

In December the new album *Their Satanic Majesties Request* was released and went gold in the United States (and later in the United Kingdom). The album was attacked, criticized, and praised by various reviewers. There were those who thought that the Stones had lost their way and predicted the demise of the group. On December 12, Brian's prison sentence was set aside because of his medical frailty, and he was placed on probation for three years, ordered to receive psychiatric care, and fined £1,000. The year ended with the Stones again having a top album, but their finances were tied up in lawsuits involving Allen Klein, Andrew Oldham, and Eric Easton. Drug use may have peaked that year, but it certainly would not disappear in the near future.

The new year started with Mick, Keith, and Brian in and out of the country. Charlie was, as always, the stable band member, home in Sussex with his wife, his jazz collection, and his American Civil War memorabilia. He was quite content. Bill was in the process of being divorced and had lost custody of his son, which depressed him greatly, but his relationship with Astrid had become very solid. Money was still a problem for all of them, despite appearances. In addition, they needed to recapture the interests of their fans and understood that they needed to return to the recording studio to produce another album.

In March the band began work on what would become *Beggars Banquet* with a number of singles. "Street Fighting Man" was Mick's attempt to show sympathy with the various youth rebellions, including the dissatisfaction with the war in Vietnam and an overall feeling toward anarchy. The band worked together on developing "Jumping Jack Flash" and a number of other songs before taking time off in April. The other large project was hiring attorneys to pursue their financial mess with Allen Klein.

At the end of May, "Jumping Jack Flash" was released as a single in the United Kingdom (a week later in the United States) and became the first number 1 hit for the Stones in two years. To premier the record and to show that they were still able to perform, the Stones made a surprise appearance at the *New Musical Express* Poll Winners Concert on May 12 in Wembley Stadium. The crowd went wild and fans had to be held back from the stage. The band received the award for best R&B group. This would be the last live performance of the Stones with Brian Jones. By their next appearance in July 1969, Brian would be dead.

During continued recordings in June, the band made "Sympathy for the Devil," and that became the centerpiece for a film by the French director Jean-Luc Godard. The filming of the song being recorded and modified was interspersed with various images created by Godard to reflect the period. The film was panned, seen as presumptuous and dull, but the Stones were seen as alive and more than a bit menacing, which gave them publicity.

This was a period of tremendous upheaval worldwide. In France, student riots began in May, and in Prague the Czech government began reforms in January that continued through August, when the Soviet Union sent in troops to crush the quiet rebellion. In April Martin Luther King was assassinated just before leading a march in Memphis. In June Robert Kennedy was assassinated after winning the California Democratic primary. And in August it seemed to all culminate with demonstrations in Chicago against the war, all during the time that the Democratic Convention was being held there. What was later termed a police riot ensued, injuring hundreds of demonstrators, many of whom were also tear gassed. The Stones anarchistic notions seemed to fit into a world reflecting uncertainty and fear.

The album was completed in June, mixing and overdubbing finished in July, but the release was delayed by the refusal of Decca to accept the cover art that the Stones wanted. Eventually the album was released with a simple white cover, but the delays carried on through November, with the album not released until December. One other issue with the album and the band was that in late May Brian was busted for drugs once again. There was fear that this would really affect interest in their new single, "Jumping Jack Flash," but there was no evidence of that as the song soared to the top of the charts. When Brian's case came to trial, he was fined but received no jail sentence.

During the summer Mick was involved with the production of a film, *Performance*, which also had Anita Pallenberg in one of the roles as a girlfriend of his. Marianne Faithfull was supposed to star as his other live-in girlfriend, but she became pregnant with Mick's child and bowed out of the filming. During that time she remained at a mansion in Ireland to be more sedate and tranquil. Unfortunately, she miscarried in the seventh month of pregnancy, in November, and the relationship between her and Mick was never quite the same again. As for the filmmaking, it was tense, raucous, and probably close to pornographic. Warner Brothers refused to release the final cut, though it finally was recut and released in 1970 to savage reviews. Since then, there has been a resurgence of interest in it, and some have even referred to it as a "classic British film."

At the end of the year Mick conceived of a television production called *The Rolling Stones Rock 'n Roll Circus Show*, which would be produced and financed by the band. They invited lots of their musical friends to participate, and those who agreed included Marianne Faithfull, John Lennon and Yoko Ono, Eric Clapton, and two other

British bands, Jethro Tull and the Who. There were also interspersed circus acts like fire-eaters, trapeze artists, and clowns. Rehearsals began on December 8 in London. The production of the show was rushed, messy, and seemed not very good in quality. Mick decided that it would not be shown or sold.

Allen Klein felt that the Stones were shown up by the Who in the latter's performance, but in retrospect, it is simply not so. The Who were presenting a new style, one that would result in their rock opera, *Tommy*. Their performance seems a bit wooden today, though it is energetic and exciting. The Stones' presentation of six numbers is still electric and spontaneous. Mick's voice is a bit tired on a couple tracks, and Brian is certainly a bit subdued, but the overall performance is great. (The DVD was made available by Allen Klein in the mid-1990s.)

The year ended with the Stones now seemingly back on track, a number 1 song, a new album that would reach number 1, and eagerness to continue to make music. Brian was, however, now almost totally shut out from the Stones, and when he was involved, his role was reduced to sidebars and instrumentation. Of course, his failure to show for rehearsals and his inability to perform most times were key factors in this situation. Charlie and Bill were also less involved, but they did not have the needs of Brian. Mick and Keith were now almost totally in charge of the band's decisions.

At the end of the year 1968 and into early 1969, Keith, Anita Pallenberg, Mick, Marianne, and her son Nicholas traveled by boat to Brazil. They relaxed on the beach and intended to search for shamans who practiced various kinds of "witchcraft" before heading into the jungles to Peru. Marianne succumbed to the heat and returned to England before the three continued on to Peru. The trip was interesting but not as fulfilling as they had hoped. During the trip, Keith and Mick did write at least two songs for the next recording session of the band, and Marianne wrote one, "Sister Morphine," about being strung out on heroin. She released the song in 1969, but it was withdrawn by Decca soon afterward because of its "likelihood to lead young people to engage in drug use."[2]

In February the band entered the recording studio and began laying down initial tracks for their new album. They also pressed a single, "Honky Tonk Women" (written in South America), and "You Can't Always Get What You Want," released as a double A side in July. Both went to number 1 in the United States and the United Kingdom and remained on the charts for more than 15 weeks. The album recordings would spread out over nine months. Brian would play on two songs, "You Got the Silver" (autoharp) and "Midnight Ramble" (congas). He was back in the clinic for depression, however, missing a number of rehearsals.[3]

Recording sessions were also thrown off by the arrest of Mick and Marianne on May 28. Officers with a search warrant came into their home, found about a quarter ounce of marijuana, and charged them, but Mick claimed Marianne was not involved and took the fall. He was fined £200 after being convicted of possession of the drug on December 19. Despite this action against him, Mick felt that Brian's lack of reliability and drug record imperiled both their recording and their ability to tour since it was unlikely he would be allowed to enter the United States while on three years' probation.

Thus Mick, after many efforts to aid Brian, decided that he should be removed from the group and presented his plan to the other Stones. Keith supported it. Neither Charlie nor Bill objected, and Mick recruited Mick Taylor, a young guitarist, to play on the album being cut. At the end of May or early in June (accounts vary),

In June 1969 Mick Jagger and Marianne Faithfull leave after a London court appearance for marijuana possession. (AP-690623087)

Keith and Mick, accompanied by Charlie, drove to Brian's home to give him the news of his dismissal. He seemed relieved to be rid of the strain, at least initially, though he was said to have cried all night after the three left. The news was not released until about June 8, though rumors preceded the official announcement from the Stones' office.

Brian was the most popular Stone after Mick, and they knew that the band had to do something dramatic to regain the fans' popularity after Brian's ignominious dumping. After seeing Blind Faith (Eric Clapton, Stevie Winwood, Ginger Baker, and Rich Grech) give a free concert in Hyde Park, Mick decided that a similar free concert of the Rolling Stones in Hyde Park would ramp up interest and gratefulness toward the Stones, and he set a date of July 5 for such a performance.

For most of June the band either rehearsed or recorded. On July 2, a very humid day and night, Brian had friends over for dinner at his home outside London. They went out to the pool later, but only Brian and Frank Thoroughgood, the general contractor for renovations to be done at Brian's home, swam at all. Brian had been drinking and taking sleeping pills and was unsteady; he was also having asthma problems. Frank went in for a cigarette, and when the women discovered that Brian was out there alone, they went outside to find he was motionless at the bottom of the pool. The three managed to get him out and tried to revive him but were unsuccessful. He was dead at the age of 27. There were questions about the circumstances of his death, but despite many thinking it suspicious, it was ruled accidental, "death by misadventure." Brian had recently broken up with his girlfriend, and his new girlfriend simply hadn't realized that like a small child, it was dangerous to leave Brian alone. His carelessness and sense of self-destructiveness were too risky. (On August 31, 2009, British police announced that they were reopening an investigation into Brian Jones's death, after rumors of foul play lingered after 40 years.)

Brian's death shocked the band as well as rock fans throughout the world. Coming just three days before the Stones' free concert in Hyde Park, it made the event far more somber. Tributes to Brian's musical genius poured into London, and each of the Stones spoke of his spirit, abilities, and friendship. More than 500 attended the funeral in Cheltenham on July 10. Charlie and Bill were there with their partners, but Mick and Marianne were filming in Australia. Keith, Anita, Allen, Klein, and Andrew were notable by their absence.

As for the concert, between 250,00 and 500,000 were estimated to have come to the park to hear the various acts on Saturday, July 5. It was a hot, muggy day, and the Stones, who were scheduled to come on stage at 5:30 P.M., would close the show. Mick began with a tribute to Brian, a reading of a poem by Percy Bysshe Shelley, the great 17th-century British poet. Then, after a moment of silent remembrance, the park was plunged into the sounds of rock and roll. The Stones' first concert in 14 months was less than an hour, but they played songs from *Beggars Banquet*, the upcoming album (*Let It Bleed*), and a few old standards like "Satisfaction." The Stones were back, but they would never be the same.

The Stones returned to the studio in the fall, after Mick returned from Australia and the filming of *Ned Kelly*. Before he departed for Australia, however, he began a long affair with Marsha Hunt, an African American singer and actress living in England. Though they would never live together, she was the mother of Mick's first child, a daughter named Karis, born in 1970.

During the hiatus from recording, the world had experienced some amazing events. The first men landed on the moon on July 20. The Woodstock rock festival took place in Bethel, New York, in mid-August, seen by some as the peak of the youth revolution. Unknown at that time was the secret American bombing of Cambodia, which began in March and extended into 1970. This was part of President

The Stones perform at a free concert (termed a tribute to Brian Jones) before more than 250,000 in Hyde Park, London, for the first time in two years on July 5, 1969, just days after Jones's death. (AP-690705088)

Nixon's secret plan to end the war in Vietnam, which only heightened tensions and accelerated the antiwar movement.

With most of the recording finished for the next album, which would be *Let It Bleed,* the Stones were eager to return to the road and tour. This would be the first tour with Mick Taylor, born in 1949, who debuted with John Mayall's Blues Breakers band at 16 and joined the Stones at 20, playing a dual lead guitar with Keith. The band was eager to get him on the road with them. They first flew to Los Angeles in mid-October to prepare for the tour for three weeks. This would be the first tour where the Stones brought all their own equipment for staging the concert. The improved and large amplifiers, the large stage, and the backdrops would all be the same from venue to venue, and the venues would be similar, large arenas. The stage set would become a kind of second home for the next two months.

On November 7 the band flew to Colorado State University in Fort Collins for the first show. Terry Reid, then B.B. King opened, as they would on a number of the shows, as well as Ike and Tina Turner, who were not in Ft. Collins. The reaction to the Stones was somewhat subdued, and Mick Jagger thought the crowd was simply too stoned to move. The next day there were two shows at the Forum in Los Angeles, received with more enthusiasm, then a show at the Oakland Coliseum. These were all venues with seating of 15,000 to 20,000.

San Diego; Phoenix; Dallas; Auburn, Alabama; Champaign, Illinois; Chicago; Los Angeles (again, where they taped songs for the *Ed Sullivan Show*); Detroit; Philadelphia; and Baltimore comprised the rest of the itinerary, achieved over the next two weeks before the band arrived in New York City. By this time the rust from not playing publicly for more than a year had worn off; the Stones were rocking and getting great reviews. There were some personal disappointments. Marianne, still in London, had run off to Rome with an Italian artist. Mick was crushed, more because he was embarrassed at being dumped than anything else. Despite this, the tour was going well, and the Stones wanted to do something that would reflect their gratefulness as well as look good. Thus they decided on another free concert to end the tour, this to be a week after the official end of the tour and in San Francisco. They proposed to have it in Golden Gate Park and to have a number of other acts, most notably the Grateful Dead, also perform. They engaged their managers to work with officials in San Francisco to make it happen.

Meanwhile, the concerts at Madison Square Garden in New York went off on November 27 and 28 (two shows). At a press conference at the Rainbow Room in New York, Mick revealed the plan for the free concert, designed in part to offset the criticism about the sky-high prices for the concerts.

Following New York, the Stones did two shows the next day in Boston Garden, then the final show tour on November 30 in Palm Beach, Florida. They then went to Muscle Shoals, Alabama, to record cuts for what would be the next album, *Sticky Fingers*.

Negotiations for the free concert continued, now handled by the Stones' local representative, celebrity lawyer Melvin Belli. The city, fearing rioting or excessive damage, refused to issue a permit for the concert in Golden Gate Park, which set Belli scrambling to find a venue for the concert, now set for December 6. After losing a couple more locations, agreement was reached to perform at the Altamont Speedway in Livermore, California, about 20 miles east of Oakland in the East Bay.[4]

There were many problems with the site; it was much smaller than needed and the access roads were limited, but the concert was set to be there anyway. Other acts scheduled were Santana; Jefferson Airplane; Crosby, Stills, Nash, and Young; the Flying Burrito Brothers; and the Grateful Dead. The concert organization was disastrous. Because the venue was not approved until the Thursday before the Saturday concert, there was a tremendous amount to do, and some things were not fully addressed or thought out.

One of the most crucial issues was security. The stage was only four feet high, much lower than the seven foot minimum at other concerts. With innumerable prior incidents of fans climbing onto the stage, there was a need for better security of some sort. In discussions with members of the Grateful Dead, it was suggested that the Hell's Angels motorcycle gang might be used to protect the stage. This resonated with Mick because an affiliate of sorts had provided some security at the free concert in Hyde Park in July, and there had been no incidents.

The local Hells Angels chapter, led by a man named Sonny Barger, was approached, and they said that they didn't do security. Pushed a bit, they agreed to sit up or around the stage as deterrents in exchange for being supplied with beer. Initially this seemed sufficient, but as the audience got ramped up on various drugs, including alcohol, and the Angels did the same, relations between the two became tenser and nastier. The Angels wielded sawed-off pool cues, with lead weights for heft, to beat back fans. The Angels also became incensed when attendees touched or pushed against their motorcycles, setting off another round of yelling, threats, and whacking.

In a full-length film made about the concert, titled *Gimme Shelter*, it is evident that the fans were becoming difficult to control long before the Stones arrive by helicopter. Hundreds of cars had been abandoned on the road and people hiked over the hills into the raceway. There were too few toilets, and in one early melee, one of the members of the Jefferson Airplane, Marty Balin, was knocked unconscious by a member of the Hells Angels. At hearing this, the Grateful Dead decided that they would not perform and left the premises.

The Stones arrived at dusk, and as they started to perform, fans kept jumping up on the stage and rushing them. The band stopped and started songs a number of times. Then, during the playing of "Under My Thumb," a young man named Meredith Hunter tried to approach the stage with a handgun. He seemed under the influence of some substance and, seeing the gun, a member of the Angels stabbed him repeatedly, and other Angels chased him down and repeatedly kicked him in the head. The incident is gruesomely captured on the film. The young man was finally reached by medical personnel but died before reaching the hospital. The Stones finished their set but were visibly shaken by all that occurred. They flew out immediately.

The ugliness and death of the Altamont concert were seen as the low point of a youth and peace movement that seemed to peak only four months previously at Woodstock. Social situations also were becoming more frayed. In November 1969, over 250,000 marchers descended on Washington, D.C., to march in protest of the war in Vietnam, while President Nixon bunkered himself in the White House.

A year that had started with such promise for the Stones had ended in a tragic death, after the earlier tragedy involving Brian Jones and the various drug arrests and domestic breakups. The Stones had produced great music, culminating in the release of *Let It Bleed* in December. The album went multiplatinum in the United States and was the number 1 album in the United Kingdom. Two of the singles also topped the charts, and their compilation album, *Through the Past Darkly*, reached number 1, also. The Rolling Stones were back as the greatest rock and roll band in the world, but to some, also one of evil. These would be descriptions that would be carried by them for quite a while. The new year, with a new group member and new relationships, would be a time to modify or reinforce those images.

NOTES

1. See Christopher Andersen (1993), *Jagger, Unauthorized,* New York: Delacorte Press, pp. 234–35; Kris Needs (2004), *Keith Richards: Before They Make Me Run,* London: Plexus, p. 135; Stephen Davis (2001), *Old Gods Almost Dead: The 40-Year Odyssey of the Rolling Stones,* New York: Broadway Books, p. 357; Bill Wyman, with Richard Havers (2002), *Rolling with the Stones,* London: DK, p. 384.
2. See Marianne Faithfull, with David Dalton (1994), *Faithfull: An Autobiography,* New York: Cooper Square Press, p. 167.
3. Bill Wyman, with Ray Coleman (1990), *Stone Alone: The Story of a Rock 'n Roll Band,* New York: Viking, p. 516.
4. Details of this are well documented through the film Albert Maysles and David Maysles (Directors) (1994), *Gimme Shelter,* filmed in 1970.

CHAPTER FIVE

The Stones Look to Top Themselves (Again): The Stones in the Early 1970s

After a triumphant tour was marred by the tragedy of Altamont, the Stones spent most of 1970 getting reacquainted. Mick Taylor, just 20 years old, would want to play more with the band in preparation for another album, whenever that might be. Mick Jagger, after being left by Marianne Faithfull while he was on tour, managed to convince her to return to him, after which he fell back into the same behavior that had led her to leave. He continued his latest affair with Marsha Hunt as well as seeing many other women. He professed love for Marianne but then ignored her as much as possible, so it seemed. She became more and more involved with drugs after the stillborn birth of their child and Mick's treatment of her.[1]

Keith and Anita had a son, Marlon, and that made Mick a bit envious. He and Marsha Hunt agreed to try to have a child, and their daughter, Karis, was born in November, though Mick failed to support her, denying that he was the father, until two successful paternity suits were brought against him. Despite their parenthood, both Anita and Keith were becoming more involved with drugs. Anita discovered heroin, and soon afterward, Keith was also using it regularly.[2] Charlie and Bill remained the drug-free members of the band as well as the most domesticated. Bill, after dozens of affairs and a broken marriage, tried to be a good partner to Astrid

Lundstrom, while Charlie was steadfast in his love and loyalty to his wife, Shirley.

One major alteration in the band was their switch from Decca Records to Atlantic, where they were to have their own label as part of the deal with Ahmet Ertegun, the founder of the company. The previous summer, Mick had contacted Ertegun when the Stones were recording in Los Angeles and Ertegun was also in California on other business. Mick had said that the band's contract with Decca was up and that they wanted to switch to Atlantic. Ertegun was excited but also tired from a long day, and it was way after midnight when they met at a club. Ertegun fell asleep, which actually impressed Mick since he hated pushy people. The next day the band and Ertegun met again and began negotiating a contract, one that lasted 15 years. It was finalized in August 1970, shortly after the band had severed their connections with Allen Klein. (Unfortunately, they signed away the rights to their 1960s music to Klein, who made millions from them, while the Stones received virtually nothing.)

Recording for the first album for their new label, Rolling Stones Records, would begin in March but become more regular, beginning in the summer. Actually the first cuts had been recorded in Muscle Shoals, Alabama, in December. There the band had recorded "Brown Sugar" (Jagger's paean to both a kind of drug and inspired by a backup singer for Ike and Tina Turner named Claudia Linnear), "Wild Horses" (inspired by Marianne's recovery from a near-death drug overdose), and "You Gotta Move." "Sister Morphine" (cowritten and initially recorded by Marianne) had been recorded in March 1969 but was held over for this new album. The rest of the album, titled *Sticky Fingers*, was recorded at the Stones' mobile recording unit, mostly located at Stargroves, Mick's country estate in East End, Newbury.

The recording sessions were interrupted by the Stones' first European tour since 1967. Most of the music would be similar to the 1969 American tour, that is, music from *Let It Bleed* and a mix of favorites from prior years. In addition, a few of the new songs, like "Wild Horses," "Dead Flowers," and "Brown Sugar," would be premiered on this tour. The tour ran six weeks, August 30 to October 9, but was only 22 shows, with no double shows in a day on this tour. The first seven shows were in the Nordic countries—three in Sweden, one in Finland, and three in Denmark—with only Copenhagen getting two shows in the same venue on consecutive nights. Generally the Stones tried to leave a day between concerts, unless they were to be in the same venue. This was different from previous tours, but now they were getting larger guarantees, the money was actually going to them (rather than managers, organizers, and promoters, a result of their new contract), the venues were consistently large, and there was no reason to risk exhaustion. The band was always drained after a show because of their intensity and their hard work. Mick became energized to the point of maniacal fervor and needed a long time to recover his equilibrium.

Four shows at different cities in Germany were followed by three shows in three days in Paris. Riots and arrests characterized many of the concert venues. The Stones brought out the rebelliousness that many young people felt, and their concerts were a good excuse, it seemed, for some to lash out. From Paris the Stones moved east to play in Vienna, then Milan and Rome, before returning to France to perform in Lyon. The tour ended with two shows in Frankfurt, one in Essen, and the closing performance in Amsterdam on October 9. The band returned to England to complete the *Sticky Fingers* album that fall.

In Paris, there had been a party after one of the concerts, and Mick was introduced to Bianca Perez-Mora Macias, a 20- (or 25, the latter is more likely) year-old Nicaraguan who had come to France to study a few years before and had lived for a time with the British actor Michael Caine. There was an attraction almost instantly, and Mick courted her in Paris, then Vienna, and finally in Rome. She returned to London with him, and in May 1971, they married when she was four months pregnant. She gave birth in October 1971 to Jade Sheena Jezebel Jagger, Mick's second daughter.

In September 1970, a live album titled *Get Yer Ya-Ya's Out!* was released in the United States and the United Kingdom. Recorded in November 1969 in Baltimore and New York, the album rose to number 1 in the United Kingdom and stayed on the charts 16 weeks. In the United States it reached number 6, was on the charts 23 weeks, and earned platinum record sales status. The record provided great financial support for the band, but even more to Decca and London (the British recording company), the last album that these companies would have with the Stones.

Following the untangling of their finances from Allen Klein, Andrew Oldham, and Eric Easton, the Stones hired new managers and accountants. After examining their finances in relation to British tax law, they were advised by their financial adviser, Prince Rupert Lowenstein,[3] to become tax exiles because of the enormous British tax rates. Thus, in March 1971, the band announced at their opening concert for the two-week British tour that they would be moving to the south of France after the tour. Mick and Keith found this exciting, while Bill was ambivalent. Charlie was quite upset since he and his wife, Shirley, had settled into quiet, comfortable country life and did not want to be uprooted. But there seemed to be no alternative. Mick Taylor, and his wife, Rose, who had no tax problems, felt compelled to move to stay close to the band.

The U.K. tour, the first since 1966, consisted of two shows at almost every stop, a total of 17 shows in 11 days (March 4–14, 1971). The 17 or so songs were drawn mostly from the new *Sticky Fingers* album as well as *Let It Bleed* and *Beggars Banquet,* with a few older songs some nights. Tour locales were Newcastle-upon-Tyne, Coventry, Manchester, Glasgow, Bristol, Brighton, Liverpool, Leeds, and two closing shows in London on March 14. Reviews indicate that the band was not good, largely because of Keith's being so drug addled, upsetting the entire rhythm of the band.[4]

There were a series of farewell parties in London before the Stones set off for France at the end of the month. Just before that, they received royalty statements and checks, which illustrated the financial split in the band. Charlie, Ian Stewart, and the estate of Brian Jones received $251 each. Bill got $662 because "In Another Land" brought him an extra $411 for writing that song. Keith and Mick each received checks for $805,000.[5]

Shortly afterward, the new album was released and went to the top of the record charts in the United States, the United Kingdom, and Australia. *Sticky Fingers* was the first album on the Rolling Stones label of Atlantic, and it had a most unusual cover, conceived by artist Andy Warhol. Depicted is a male in jeans, seen from waist to just above the knees. The "jeans" have a working zipper and, when unzipped, there are cotton briefs, rubber stamped with a warning not to photograph and the new Rolling Stones logo, giant lips with a tongue stuck out between them. Both the album cover and the songs made the album one of the top selling albums ever. This was Mick Taylor's first full album with the Stones, and the studio musicians included Nicky Hopkins on piano, Billy Preston on organ, Pete Townshend (of the Who) doing backup vocals, and Ry Cooder on slide guitar as well as a number of other famous musicians. Both "Brown Sugar" and "Wild Horses" were released as singles and remained in the charts for 12 and 8 weeks, respectively.

In France, Keith rented Villa Nellcote, a 19th-century mansion, and sublet rooms to band members. Charlie and Shirley rented a farmhouse in Provence. Bill rented a house in Grasse, as did Mick Taylor, and Mick and Bianca stayed in a hotel in St. Tropez before moving into a villa in Biot. The Stones' mobile recording studio was set up at Keith's villa, and the next album was recorded there over the summer. This was to be a double album, *Exile on Main Street,* released in May 1972. A number of the tracks for this album had actually been done at sessions in Los Angeles in 1968–1969 but never put on a record.

The band tried to work over most of June and July on the album, after everyone had attended the social event of the season, when Mick and Bianca were married on May 12, 1971, in St. Tropez, France. The guests included Eric Clapton; Paul McCartney and his wife, Linda; Ringo Starr and his wife; Keith Moon; Peter Frampton; Roger Vadim; and the entire band of the Rolling Stones. What started as a quiet wedding became a media circus, with Keith's friend and drug supplier, Tony Sanchez, providing drugs for those who needed them. Keith and Anita especially did, with their heroin addictions. Both had made halfhearted attempts to quit but were unsuccessful. The addiction would plague Keith (and thereby the band) for the rest of the decade.[6]

Mick was now firmly in charge of the band, both musically and financially, though he had a number of trusted aides who handled the day-to-day dealings. One was Prince Rupert Lowenstein, a London bank director who agreed to manage the Stones' business starting in 1970 and who did so for more than 30 years. Mick hoped to begin an American tour at the beginning of 1972 and wanted the new album completed for release and promotion at about that time. Thus there was a push through the summer to finish the recordings. Keith's heroin use, his rows with Anita, the stifling conditions in his basement where much of the recording went on, and Mick's liaisons with Marsha Hunt and Anita and Bianca all made the actual work sporadic and tedious. In addition, a number of the Stones' friends or acquaintances died from drug overdoses, accidentally or self-induced, during the summer. This did not seem to slow down the heavy drug use at Nellcote.

The result was a very unproductive summer. The band would assemble and Keith would either not be there or leave suddenly, never to return that evening. Then Mick, angry at Keith's drug use and irresponsible actions, would not show up for a few days. Mick Taylor, the newest member and the youngest, grew increasingly frustrated, confused, and finally, also fell into drug use. Charlie and

Bill continued to show up regularly but were both frustrated and felt at times marginalized by Mick and Keith.

In late October 1971, Jade Jagger was born in Paris, but the album was still not finished. Keith and Anita had caused such difficulties with the unsavory cast of characters that dropped by their villa at all hours and their well-known drug use that there were fears that the police would raid their home, and they did in November. To avoid prosecution, the entire Stones entourage moved to Los Angeles, at least temporarily. The French police were reluctant to let Keith and Anita leave, but their lawyers said that Keith would continue to rent the villa, proving that they'd return and had not really fled. Thus, for over a year, Keith paid about $2,400 a week rental while the Stones were not in France. In California, most of the work was mixing and overdubbing, and Charlie and Bill only came as needed, with Mick Jagger and Keith Richards doing most of the work and arguing a lot over that.

It took until October 1973 before the drug case was decided in court in France. Keith and Anita were fined $1,350 each and a year suspended sentence for throwing parties where drugs were used. Keith was also barred from entering France for two years, but he finally was able to stop renting the villa. Despite his financial lament about this, he was earning, at this point, about $25,000 per week with the Stones in royalties, touring, and other residuals and fees. Mick was making about the same, and the rest of the Stones less because of the extra royalties that Mick and Keith received for songwriting/composing, a sore spot with Bill, Charlie, and Mick Taylor.

The plans for the tour in the United States kept changing. The longer time to produce the *Exile on Main Street* double album was one reason. Another was the final settlement of the Allen Klein lawsuit, which was ultimately settled in March 1972 for more than $20 million, but with Klein retaining the rights to all the pre-1970 recordings. Mick felt that the next American tour would have to be in much larger venues and have much larger gate receipts after the loss of the future royalties from their 1960s music. Nevertheless, Mick was also wary, fearing that the craziness of the era might lead some unstable person to try to kill him.

In May 1972, the Stones moved to Montreux, Switzerland, to be close to the clinic where Anita was trying to wean herself from heroin. They rehearsed there for the start of the tour, set for June 1972, starting on the West Coast of North America. The new album, *Exile on Main Street,* was released in mid-May and went to number 1

in both the United Kingdom and the United States and number 2 in
Australia. Earlier, in April, the single "Tumbling Dice" had been released and gone to number 5 in the United Kingdom and number 7
in the United States, setting the stage for the new album's appearance the next month. Now the album would get fans excited about
the upcoming North American tour. After time in Montreux, the
band returned to Los Angeles to hone the playlist then set out for
Vancouver for the first date, June 3, 1972.

Exile on Main Street was composed of recordings made over a
period of four years, though most were done over summer and fall
1971. There were a total of 18 songs on two records, which included
"Tumbling Dice" and "Happy," both of which were released as singles
and did very well. The album was an immediate commercial success
but received mixed reviews from critics. Some loved it; some found
it difficult to relate to. Over the years the album has grown in stature
and is now considered by some as one of the Stones' best as well as
one of the top 100 albums ever produced.

The tour would run until July 26, and there would be 51 shows
in 54 days, with two shows in one day 12 different times. It was a
grueling schedule, and the entire tour, called the S.T.P. tour or Stones
Touring Party, was documented by a number of filmmakers and cor-
respondents who traveled on the tour. There was a tour bus, though
for some greater distances, the band would sometimes fly. There were
riots at a number of the venues as fans without tickets or (occasionally) forged tickets tried to force their way in through barricades and
phalanx of police. Tickets were being sold at 10 times their face value
since most of the shows were totally sold out. In Detroit, for example,
there were 120,000 applications for the 12,000 seats. In Montreal,
some crazed fans blew up the Stones' equipment van. The playlist for
the tour included only songs that were from 1969 forward, except
for a song like "Satisfaction" that might be used in a closing medley.
Because of an association with the Altamont tragedy, there were no
performances of "Sympathy for the Devil." For most of the concerts,
Stevie Wonder was the opening act. He had just let his Motown
contract lapse, and the exposure with this tour helped him sell his
first two independently produced and recorded albums. He often
joined the Stones for a final act medley.

The first nine shows in Vancouver, Seattle, San Francisco, Long
Beach, and the Hollywood Palladium were a bit rough, as the band
used these first shows as a type of expensive rehearsal. Starting with
the two shows at the Forum in Los Angeles, the Stones hit their stride

and wowed the audiences for the next 30 or so performances. These took the Stones from the West Coast to the Rockies (Arizona, New Mexico, and Colorado), then up into the Midwest, Texas, the South, and up the East Coast. There were four shows in San Francisco in two days and three in Chicago at the International Amphitheatre in two days. One of the largest venues was RFK Stadium in Washington, D.C., which accommodated more than 30,000 for the outdoor show. Most of the shows were indoors at large arenas seating 15,000 to 20,000. Even with that, the demand was far higher, and in a number of places, lotteries were held for tickets. Fans sent as many as 1,000 postcards, hoping that one would be drawn that allowed them to buy four tickets. After the show in Montreal on July 17, the band seemed to lose some energy, obviously from exhaustion. They were playing powerful shows and then partying in hotels and the tour buses with lots of drug use. It was not surprising that they were nearing exhaustion as they played the final shows in Boston, Philadelphia, Pittsburgh, and finally, four shows in Madison Square Garden in New York City. The temperature on stage was often 140 degrees because of the lights. There were times when Charlie could hardly hold his drumsticks because of the sweat on his hands. The band members soaked through their shirts halfway through the performances. Bill blew a number of amps in shows, three in St. Louis alone. Following the final show, which was on Mick Jagger's 29th birthday, Ahmet Ertegun hosted an enormous party for Mick and the Stones. Woody Allen, Bob Dylan, Zsa Zsa Gabor, Carly Simon, Bette Midler, Andy Warhol, Dick Cavett, and Tennessee Williams were just a few of the celebrities who attended, where the music was provided by Count Basie and his orchestra as well as the Muddy Waters Band. The final accounting for the tour showed that the 51 shows had grossed over $4 million, the richest rock tour in history. The Stones got 60 to 70 percent of that, but expenses came out of their earnings. Ultimately, each of the five Stones got about $400,000 from the tour.

Many in the entourage on the tour were amazed that the Stones could maintain their equilibrium throughout a tour where it was nearly impossible to tell one venue from the next. They almost never got out to see much, though there were side trips to the Virgin Islands in late June as well as a couple days of relaxation in the New Orleans area. Though being rock stars seemed glamorous on the outside, Charlie saw the tour as work and sleep, while Bill noted that it was just a job, though an unusual one.

Following the tour, the band members had a decision to make about where they would go. France was out since Keith and Anita's previous drug antics were still not settled there in a legal manner, still being addressed in court. British tax laws made living in the United Kingdom impossible, unless the Stones wanted to declare bankruptcy. The band members met and then went in various directions. Bill and Astrid went to Bermuda, then back to France. Mick and Bianca went to Ireland. Keith and Anita went to Switzerland. In November a number of the band members met in Venice and then, on December 4, went to Nice, France, to be questioned, individually, about Keith and Anita. It was clear that they needed a place where they could all meet without worrying about various legal issues and work on the new album that they were committed to doing for Atlantic.

The only place that would take them in (mostly because of Keith) was Jamaica, and the group arrived there in late November 1972, where they did backing tracks for the next album (*Goats Head Soup*). The band had scheduled their first tour of the Far East for January and February 1973, but there were fears that they would not be allowed to enter certain countries with the drug charges still pending. After the questioning in Nice, all the band members, but for Keith, were left uncharged. Recording went on through December 13, but the results weren't very satisfactory.

On December 23, there was a massive earthquake in Nicaragua that devastated most of the country and killed over 18,000. Mick and Bianca were in France when they saw the news on television. Since all of Bianca's relatives were still in Nicaragua, she was understandably distraught. With little communication and no scheduled airline flights going there, Mick chartered a plane, and Bianca and Mick flew to Nicaragua with all the antityphoid serum that he could obtain in England as well as other desperately needed medical supplies.

Roberto Clemente, the famous baseball player living in Puerto Rico, was also moved by this tragedy and chartered a plane to bring needed supplies to the Nicaraguans. Unfortunately, the plane was overloaded and crashed in the sea soon after takeoff from San Juan, killing Clemente.

Bianca's mother and most of her relatives had survived, but they had lost everything, as did much of the country. Mick provided money for them and got the Stones (as well as Santana and Cheech and Chong) to give a concert on January 18 in Los Angeles that raised over $500,000, all of which went to Nicaraguan relief (after expenses of about $150,000). This was the beginning of the Pacific Rim Tour.

The tour had been scheduled to visit Japan, New Zealand, and Australia, but both Japan and Australia announced that certain members of the Stones would not be allowed entry because of drug convictions. Three concerts were then scheduled in Hawaii, and these were held on January 21 and 22 (two shows). Australia ended up relenting, and the Stones were allowed to tour there, but the Japanese government held firm and the promoters had to refund ticket money to 55,000 fans who had paid for the five scheduled shows.

The band returned to Los Angeles after the Hawaii concerts and worked in the recording studio for two weeks until February 6, 1973, when they flew to Sydney. Bill Wyman thought that their playing was uneven on this tour but that the biggest problem was the weather since most of the performances were outdoors. In Brisbane they were delayed by rain; in Melbourne the temperature was nearly 100 degrees. There were nine shows in Sydney, Brisbane, Adelaide, and Perth and one in Auckland, New Zealand. The playlist included no new songs that they were recording for the next album. Immediately after the tour ended on February 27, Mick Jagger flew to Jamaica, Mick Taylor to Hong Kong, Charlie home to France, Keith to Switzerland, and Bill and Ian Stewart to Los Angeles via Hawaii. This would be the last American tour with Mick Taylor as a member of the Stones, though no one knew that at the time.

In April the Stones planned to go to Los Angeles to complete the album on which they had been working (and which would become *Goats Head Soup*), but various things got in the way, and they didn't return to California until early May. The album was finally completed and was to be released in late August to precede a tour of Europe set for September and October.

In June, Keith and Anita were busted in London at Keith's home for drugs and gun possession. In July, Redlands, Keith's home, burned, though most items were saved, other than the thatched roof. It would take years to rebuild and renovate the house. It was clear that Keith's heroin addiction was causing more problems for him as well as the rest of the Stones since he became increasingly unreliable. At the end of August the band convened in Amsterdam, where they rehearsed for 10 straight nights, then began the tour on September 1, 1973, in Vienna. *Goats Head Soup* had been released the day before and immediately rose to number 1 in the United States, the United Kingdom, and Australia before going triple platinum in the United States. "Angie" was released as a single two weeks before and went to number 1 in the United States and number 5 in the United

Kingdom and remained on the U.S. charts for 16 weeks. Album reviews were mixed, and Ian Stewart called the album "bloody insipid."

The European/U.K. tour was 49 days, and there were 42 shows with two shows on 13 different dates. There were also 19 off days in the 49, so there was some time for the band to relax. There were 21 cities visited in eight countries, and over 300,000 fans attended the concerts. Gross receipts were over $600,000, and the net was around $400,000. All the shows were sold out, and tickets were being scalped at 10 to 20 times their face value. The tour rolled from Austria to West Germany to London, playing sport halls or large stadia like Wembley. Then it was Manchester, Glasgow, and Birmingham before returning to the Continent to play in Innsbruck, Austria; Switzerland, Munich, West Germany; Copenhagen and Aarhus, Denmark; Gothenburg, Sweden; Essen, West Germany; Rotterdam; Antwerp, Brussels; and a closing concert in West Berlin. (Germany was not united until 1989–1990.)

As the tour ended, Keith was found guilty and fined in France and found guilty of lesser drug and firearms charges in England and fined; Anita paid a fine for the French charges and had the equivalent of probation for the British charges. Keith denied to newspapers that drugs were affecting his life or his work, but they clearly were, as later events would prove.[7]

The band convened in Munich in November 1973 to do recordings at Musicland Studios. Ronnie Wood of the Faces joined them for some sessions. Rumors had flown that claimed the Stones and the Faces would be combining, with Rod Stewart going off on his own. The latter did occur, but there was no joining of forces between the two bands. "Woody" had gotten very close to Mick and Keith and had even recorded a version of "It's Only Rock 'n Roll" at Wood's house in July, joined by Kenny Jones and Ian McLagen of the Faces. Ultimately, Wood would join the band, but that was another year in the future. Bill went to Los Angeles to record his own solo work since he felt he'd never be able to get anything written and recorded with the Stones. Wyman's album, *Monkey Grip,* came out in May 1974, the first solo album by a Rolling Stone. It would not be the last.

Not long afterward, Keith began working more closely with Ronnie Wood, and they formed a project that they called the New Barbarians, which ultimately led to concert appearances in 1979. Yet the Rolling Stones were still together, and after the recording in Munich, work continued into 1974. After successfully producing *Beggars Banquet, Let It Bleed,* and *Goats Head Soup,* Jimmy Miller was dropped by Mick for the new album. Instead he and Keith, as the Glimmer Twins, were the producers of *It's Only Rock and Roll.*

The album was released in October 1974, reaching number 1 in the United States and number 2 in the United Kingdom. All songs were credited to Jagger and Richards, although Mick Taylor had provided significant input on at least two of the songs. Taylor was annoyed at this slight as well as other lost opportunities to have his work produced and played by the Stones, much as Bill Wyman had been bothered by similar actions. Bill had just had his own work produced independently and released on the Rolling Stone label. Mick Taylor, however, had other reasons for becoming disenchanted with his work as a Rolling Stone. He had gotten into much heavier drug use, specifically heroin, and his wife, Rose, thought that Mick (Taylor) was becoming sexually involved with Mick Jagger. Taylor thought that he was being strained too much, was losing touch with reality, and that Mick Jagger was coming on to Rosie, Mick Taylor's wife. So in December 1974, he abruptly announced that he was quitting the Stones. Bill empathized, Charlie understood, and Mick Jagger was hurt. Keith was angry because the band was about to begin work in the studio on a new album and Keith thought that this would set them back. Keith's selfish view was typical of him during his heroin addiction phase.[8]

Mick Taylor had joined the Stones when he was 20 and had been the baby to the older Stones, who were all at least six years older than he. Certainly they had all been that young when the band started, but times and situations were different. Mick Taylor was closed out of some things and pressured into others because of the band culture. No one doubted his musical competence; in fact the Stones all praised him to the heights when he announced his departure. Still he felt in need of splitting, though he never did find the same success outside the band that he had enjoyed in it. Nevertheless he had resigned, and there was a need to fill his spot. When and how that was to be done would be up to the remaining Stones, but more Mick Jagger than anyone else.

The band went back to rehearsing and recording in Munich with the four remaining band members plus Nicky Hopkins, a keyboardist who had recorded with them on recent albums. Speculation on who would replace Mick Taylor was a common topic in the music media. But at the end of the year, no decisions had been made.

The Rolling Stones in rehearsal in December 1969 before a London concert: from left, Mick Taylor, Charlie Watts, Mick Jagger, Keith Richards, and Bill Wyman. (AP-6912140107)

In January 1975, Mick, Keith, Charlie, Bill, and Billy Preston, who had been doing a lot of touring and session work with the Stones, went to Rotterdam, where they would try out guitarists. Of the three top guitarists who jammed with the band, none seemed to have what was being sought, that is, a good enough fit. At the end of March, in Munich, they had another try with some guitarists, but none seemed right until, on April 1, Ron Wood came and sat in with the Stones. The chemistry was perfect, and the guitar playing was good enough, so the group agreed to offer him a membership as a Stone. The official announcement to the press was April 14, 1975, wherein it was noted that Ron Wood would accompany the Stones on their tour of North and South America, slated to begin in June 1975. It was to be just a temporary joining, for the tour. Wood would still be part of the Faces.

At the end of April the band arrived in New York City, staying at two different hotels under assumed names. They came to rehearse and promote the upcoming tour. Despite the seemingly mundane arrival, there had been some question as to whether Keith would even be allowed in the country because of his conviction for heroin possession. Mick went to a friend that he had made at some of the parties that he attended that had included royalty like Princess Margaret, the queen's sister. According to Tony Sanchez, Keith's friend, confidant, and drug procurer, Mick went to Walter Annenberg, the U.S. ambassador to Great Britain, with a request to help get Keith a visa for the tour. Annenberg came back to say that if Keith would undergo a blood test and no trace of heroin was found in his blood, he would receive a visa. Keith went to Switzerland where a year before he had had his blood cleansed in an experimental medical procedure that removed his blood and replaced it with unblemished blood. It was part of a heroin withdrawal cure, which had worked for a time. The procedure was done once again, and then Keith flew back to England, where he was given a blood test at the American embassy. When the physician's verdict was negative, his visa was stamped, and the tour was able to go on. Keith now denies this story as a complete legend. The insinuation is that Mick contributed a large sum of money to the Pan American Fund (very close to Annenberg's heart), and this greased the wheels with immigration.[9]

After rehearsing for four days, on May 1 the Stones rented a flatbed truck, put a stage on it with their instruments, and performed live on the truck as it rolled down New York's 5th Avenue from 12th Street all the way to Washington Square, at the end of 5th. They gave a press conference and excited thousands of fans, who chased the truck down the street. On May 18 the band flew to Newburg, New York, about 50 miles north of the city, where their stage set had been assembled in an aircraft hangar, and rehearsed there for five days. They went back to Long Island to relax, then returned to Newburg, where they boarded a chartered Boeing 727 and flew to New Orleans. They bused to Baton Rouge, where the tour began on the campus of Louisiana State University, with two shows on June 1.

This tour (The Tour of the Americas '75) was even bigger than the prior North American swing, done in 1972. The band did 45 shows in 26 cities in 21 states (plus the District of Columbia and Toronto, Ontario) in 69 days. Over a million fans saw the performances, and the tour grossed over $10 million. The stage was designed like a lotus flower with five giant petals that went out into the audience. At some point in the show, a giant (20-foot-long) inflatable penis emerged from a hole in the stage and Mick proceeded to ride it around suggestively before it disappeared again into the stage. The playlist was mostly newer numbers, with a few songs from the 1960s. Venues were often football or baseball stadiums seating 50,000 or more. That was the case in Milwaukee, Kansas City, Cleveland, Dallas, Jacksonville, and Buffalo, with the remaining venues being large basketball arenas of at least 15,000.

The tour was scheduled to extend into Mexico and South America, with four shows in Mexico City; four in Rio de Janeiro, Brazil; four in Sao Paulo, Brazil; and four in Caracas, Venezuela, all between August 10 and 31, but civil unrest and currency fluctuations caused that to be canceled. To accompany the Americas tour, Rolling Stones Records released a greatest hits package, titled *Made in the Shade,* with 10 songs from the previous three albums. The album went to number 6 in the United States and remained on the charts for nine weeks, while in the United Kingdom it reached number 14 but was on the charts for 12 weeks.

After the tour ended, both Bill and Mick Jagger went off to work on solo record projects, Bill in California and Mick in Toronto. Charlie returned to his home in England. Keith met Anita in Los Angeles. In late October, most of the Stones went to Montreux, Switzerland, to work on overdubs for the new album that had been recorded in Munich. In November, at a meeting in Geneva, the band (minus Keith, who never showed up) determined to go on tour in the United Kingdom and Europe in summer 1976, their first tour there since 1973. Peter Rudge, who had organized the last two tours for the Stones and was now acting as their spokesperson, would do the logistics for the tour. In December, Mick and Bianca went to Rio for Christmas, then returned to find an apartment in New York City. The bigger news in December was that the Faces had agreed to break up as a group. That left Ronnie Wood to join the Rolling Stones as a permanent member, and that officially became the case in February 1976. It was the beginning of a new Stones era, one that would last much longer than anyone, even the Stones, anticipated.

NOTES

1. Marianne Faithfull discusses her extensive drug use and the consequences of that in her 1994 autobiography with David Dalton, *Faithfull: An Autobiography,* New York: Cooper Square Press. Chapters 6 and 7 deal with this period in her life with and without Jagger.
2. Keith and Anita's extensive drug use is discussed by Kris Needs (2004), *Keith Richards: Before They Make Me Run,* London: Plexus, as well as by Stephen Davis (2001), *Old Gods Almost Dead: The 40-Year Odyssey of the Rolling Stones,* New York: Broadway Books, pp. 349–62, but the most

extensive examination is by Robert Greenfield (2006), *Exile on Main Street: A Season in Hell with the Rolling Stones*, Cambridge, MA: Da Capo Press.

3. Lowenstein's family had a conferred title of "prince" from Belgium's era of royalty in the 1700s. The title he held was only an honorary title but was legitimate.

4. Reviews of the time and later books speak specifically to Keith's slurred ability on the guitar, which threw off the tempo of the band.

5. Bill Wyman, with Richard Havers (2002), *Rolling with the Stones*, London: DK, p. 273.

6. Discussed extensively by Davis, *Old Gods Almost Dead;* Stanley Booth (1985), *The True Adventures of the Rolling Stones,* New York: Vintage Books; Needs, *Keith Richards;* Christopher Andersen (1993), *Jagger, Unauthorized,* New York: Delacorte Press; Philip Norman (1984), *Symphony for the Devil,* New York: Linden Press/Simon and Schuster; Greenfield, *Exile on Main Street.*

7. See Needs, *Keith Richards,* and Greenfield, *Exile on Main Street.*

8. See Davis, *Old Gods Almost Dead*, pp. 391–92.

9. See Tony Sanchez (1979), *Up and Down with the Rolling Stones,* New York: William Morrow, p. 293.

CHAPTER SIX

The Stones Reinvented: Ronnie Wood Is a Permanent Fixture, but Keith?

The biggest Stones news, as 1975 turned to 1976, was that Ron Wood, "Woody," would be a permanent fixture with the Stones. Though not the best of the best guitarists, he was an excellent musician, and his personality fit well with the band. He was especially close to Keith, which was good since he and Mick were moving apart, partly because of Mick's greater comfort with a more "royal" crowd but also because of Keith's continued heroin addiction, despite his half-hearted efforts to quit. As long as Anita was addicted and she and Keith were together, Keith would be unable to quit his heroin use.

The Stones had started recordings in early 1975 in Rotterdam and Munich for their new album. Then they continued sessions in Munich and Montreux in late 1975 and, finally, finished recording in New York at Atlantic Studios in early 1976. Plans were made for a European tour for late spring 1976, rather than summer, as first envisioned, the first on the Continent since the U.K./European tour of fall 1973. The plans were not without some peril, however.

In February Mick was admitted to a hospital in New York, suffering from a drug overdose of indeterminate origin. He stayed only overnight, leaving once the media had picked up on the story. Despite the overdose, Mick and Bianca were out most nights, usually at Studio 54, a club with a large jet set following and where drugs were readily available and used. New York was the center of this decadent partying in the late 1970s, just as London had claimed the dubious distinction in the late 1960s. This time, however, there was the additional danger of AIDS, and a number of the Stones' friends and acquaintances became victims of the disease, most notably the bisexuals or homosexuals and the intravenous drug users.[1] Though all the Stones knew these people, Mick and Bianca were most integrally involved with them.

In April the new album, *Black and Blue,* was released, first in the United States, then a week later in the United Kingdom. It rose to number 1 in the United States, remaining there for 4 weeks and in the charts for 14 weeks, and number 2 in the United Kingdom, also remaining on the charts for 14 weeks. The album had only eight songs, the fewest of any Stones album. There are a variety of musical genres on the album, with heavy doses of funk amid the small number of songs. As planned, it came out just before the tour, with five of the eight songs on the tour play list. Despite the excellent sales, the album did not receive universal critical acclaim. In fact, there were and are those who decry this album as well as *Goats Head Soup* and *It's Only Rock and Roll.* Robert Palmer, the noted music writer and friend of both Keith Richards and Ron Wood, said that those three albums "were what the Rolling Stones sounded like with Keith preoccupied and the others bored and dispirited."[2]

The tour began on April 28 in Frankfurt, West Germany. Rehearsals had been scheduled for April 11 in the south of France. Because of late arrivals, the start date was pushed back a day, but after a week, Keith still hadn't arrived. He was finally allowed back into France, but that seemed not to have affected his timeliness. He finally showed up on April 19, but rehearsals went very poorly and they didn't improve much, even as they finished and the Stones headed to Frankfurt.

Concert performance reviews were very uneven, often savage, but the demand for tickets was higher than it had ever been. The demand was so great for the three shows scheduled for London that three more shows were added. This was still not enough to meet the enormous demand, but it did make some fans much happier. The band would do a total of 41 shows in 57 days, with two shows in one day only twice (Munster in April and Cologne in early June). The enormous stage took 14 people to construct at each venue and that, and travel time, seemed to dictate days off for the Stones while on tour. After Frankfurt, there were concerts in northern Germany (Munster, Kiel, West Berlin, Bremen), then two shows in Brussels before the band went on to the United Kingdom. Besides the six shows in London, there were performances in Glasgow (three), Leicester (two), and Stafford (two).

On May 18 Keith was involved in an auto accident while driving his Bentley from the Stafford venue to his home. There were four others in the car, including his son Marlon. Keith fell asleep at the wheel, and the car left the M1 motorway and ended up in a field. When taken to the station house, drugs were found on his person, and he was charged with possession once again. Eight months later, he was found guilty of cocaine and LSD possession and fined just under $2,000.

From the United Kingdom the tour went to The Hague, Holland, then to Cologne and Dortmund in Germany, before four shows in Paris and one in Lyon. The Stones gave their first concert ever in Spain on June 11 in Barcelona, then moved on to Nice and Zurich before concerts in southern Germany in Munich and Stuttgart. The tour ended with two shows in Zagreb (then part of Yugoslavia, now located in Croatia), their first concerts in Eastern Europe since the concert in Warsaw in 1967. The tour closed with a show in Vienna. The reviews were the worst that they had ever received.

In early June Keith's life was again the source of tragedy as his infant son Tara, just 10 weeks old, suffocated in his crib in Geneva, Switzerland. Despite their sorrow, the band performed that night, as scheduled, in Paris, and Anita joined the tour directly after that. The continuing heroin use of both Anita and Keith was exacerbated by the sudden death of their young son. Things would get worse within the year.[3]

In late August the Stones were one of a half dozen acts scheduled to appear at the Knebworth Fair. Begun in 1974 in the village of Knebworth (about 25 miles north of London), and continuing most years since then, the fair in 1976 was seen by many as the potential site of the Stones' last concert before they dissolved. Keith's continued troubles and growing acrimony toward him, even from Mick, made some observers see the breakup as inevitable and imminent. There were also fears that Keith would not live much longer unless he was able to find a cure for his continued addiction. Thus over 150,000 people arrived for the concert, where the Stones played from 11:30 P.M. to 2:00 A.M., performing more than 25 numbers.

The rumors were wrong. The Stones were not breaking up, despite Keith's problems, and in February 1977, they agreed to a new contract with Atlantic Records (for the United States and Canada) and EMI (for the rest of the world). A plan for the next album was that it would be a live album, drawn from the tour of the Americas in 1975, the European tour of 1976, and recordings made at a club (El Mocambo) in Toronto in March.

The band got together in Toronto in mid-February for rehearsals at a film studio in the suburb of Lakeshore. The El Mocambo dates were set for March 4 and 5, but with no prior publicity. The band was to take over part of the scheduled playing dates of a Canadian group, April Wine. The Stones were listed on the publicity bill as "The Cockroaches," but rumors abounded and the club was packed for the performances.

The band had begun rehearsing in February with Keith and Billy Preston, who had toured with them on the last two tours and had played on a number of their albums. Keith arrived in Canada almost a week later than the rest of the band. On entering the country, Keith and Anita were stopped at customs and searched. Not surprisingly, drugs were found in Anita's bag, and she was charged with possession of hashish and heroin. At the hotel, Keith went directly to bed and got up for a rehearsal session at 4:30 A.M. He returned to the Harbour Castle Hotel and to bed, but at 4:30 P.M. on Sunday, February 27, Canadian drug officers raided Anita and Keith's suite at the hotel. Keith was asleep, but in a pouch next to the bed was an ounce of top-quality heroin. Both he and Anita were arrested and released on bail after their passports were confiscated. Having such an amount of heroin subjected Keith to a charge of trafficking, which carried a life sentence in prison. Keith's life as a free man and the band's continued existence now hung in the balance.

Anita had been charged with simple possession and pleaded guilty on March 4. The band decided to play that evening at El Mocambo, which could accommodate 300 people. Keith was ill from withdrawal, and Bill and Woody managed to score some heroin for him since going cold turkey was impossible. When the band headed for the club that evening, another issue arose as Mick took Margaret Trudeau, the 29-year-old wife of the Canadian prime minister, in his limousine to the club. The Trudeaus had been having marital issues, and some of it was related to the fact that she had married at age 22, while her husband was 51. Often she wanted to "act her age," and this was one of those times, as she was thrilled to be with the Rolling Stones entourage. Her timing was particularly poor, considering the other problems that were evident for the band at that time. Ultimately,

Margaret Trudeau would check into the Harbour Castle Hotel and hang out with the Stones for the rest of their stay in Toronto, attending both shows at El Mocambe and supposedly having brief affairs with Mick and then Ronnie Wood.[4] When the Stones departed for New York, so did she, and the press was quite aware of it. Trudeau said that she was in New York for a long-planned vacation. There were some in Canada who thought that the prime minister should resign over his wife's actions, but nothing more came of it, and Margaret returned to her husband by the end of March.

Both nights of playing at El Mocambo were recorded, and the following day the Stones listened to the tapes to voice their views on which numbers might be included in the new, live album. Keith made a brief court appearance that same day and was scheduled for a full hearing on March 14, a week later. One by one, the Stones left for New York, but Keith could not, and on March 14 Anita's trial led to two small fines. Keith, however, had a full trial date set for June 27. By that date Keith would have to kick the habit if he were to have any chance at a lenient or positively creative sentence.

After a meeting of the band with Jane Rose, a personal assistant to Keith, it was agreed that Keith had to go into a serious rehab program. On April 1 Richards was granted admission into the United States to enter into rehab at a clinic in New Jersey. When his trial came up on June 27, he failed to appear in court, and his lawyer explained that he was taking a cure for addiction. His case was postponed until a new trial date, December 2, 1977.

The Stones didn't do much that summer as a band, with Keith in rehab. In mid-September 1977, the new live album, *Love You Live,* came out in the United Kingdom and the United States and rose to number 3 in the United Kingdom and a listing on the charts for eight weeks and number 5 in the United States with seven weeks on the charts. The album was produced by the Glimmer Twins (Mick and Keith). The Stones came to New York at that time to promote the album, and Keith managed to join them for a photo session and seemed to be addiction-free and much thinner, according to Bill Wyman.[5]

During the summer, rumors of Mick and Bianca ending their marriage were rampant and hotly denied, but in October Mick arrived at Bill's 41st birthday party in Paris with an American model, with whom he was obviously more than just a friend. He and Jerry Hall had met in May 1976 but had only become close in summer 1977, when they had attended a flashy birthday party for

The Rolling Stones appear at Trax Music Club in New York City in September 1977 to promote their new live album, Love You Live: *from left, Charlie Watts, Mick Jagger, Keith Richards, Ronnie Wood, and Bill Wyman. (AP-770923048)*

designer Diane von Furstenberg at New York's 21 Club. It was clear to many (including Mick) that his marriage was broken. The only question was how long it would be maintained legally. (The marriage was officially dissolved with a divorce decree in England on November 5, 1980.)

The Stones had located themselves in Paris and began recording sessions at studios there in the second week of October 1977. They worked on recording until the end of November. This was an important time for the Stones. First there had been the rumors of a breakup. Then Keith's drug problems made the possibility of a breakup even more likely. Finally, there were critics in the music industry who saw the Stones as dinosaurs. They had been together more than 15 years, and it seemed that they were not going to adjust to changing public interests in music. The Stones were eager to show that all these rumors and concerns were not true.

Recording continued in Paris in December for a couple weeks then after Christmas, during the end of January 1978. At Keith's trial in December his lawyer refuted the trafficking charge by submitting bank statements and living expenses. Clearly there was no need to traffic. Still, the charge of possession of heroin remained.

Keith's trial was finally held in October 1978, and he pleaded guilty to heroin possession. He was given a suspended sentence and put on probation for a year with orders to continue treatment for heroin addiction. In addition, he had agreed to put on two benefit concerts that would include the Rolling Stones and the New Barbarians that were to be held in Oshawa, Ontario, Auditorium, which seated just under 4,000. The agreement to do this may have been what tipped the Canadian scales of justice in his favor. The suggestion actually came from a young lady whom Keith met on an earlier tour. According to Keith he gave a blind girl named Rita Bedard a ride at least once and befriended her (he called her his blind angel). On her own, the young woman went to the judge's house and spoke of the kindness and thoughtfulness of Keith Richards. Impressed, the judge modified his sentence as a result of the young woman's intervention. This has always been the story, but later writing makes much of this account questionable and credits the judge with independently suggesting the concert.[6] Nevertheless, Keith would not go to jail.

Keith's problems were matched to some degree by those of Mick and Ronnie, both of whom were being sued for divorce. The new album, *Some Girls,* was due for a June 1978 release. In May a single from the forthcoming album was released. "Miss You" was an immediate hit, rising to number 1 in the United States, staying on the charts for 20 weeks, and to number 3 in the United Kingdom, while on the charts for seven weeks. Four singles from the album also were listed in the charts.

Almost simultaneously, the Stones began a U.S. tour and had the new album released. The tour hyped the album and the album gave the tour higher demand. The album rose to number 1 in the United States (number 2 in the United Kingdom) and stayed on the charts for 32 weeks in the United States (25 in the United Kingdom), the longest run for a Stones album since 1971 (*Sticky Fingers*). The tour playlist had 5 of the 10 songs from the album performed at each venue, with a sixth done occasionally.

The rumors of the band's demise were clearly wrong, and the Stones wanted to have a smashing tour to lay those critical comments to rest for good. They began rehearsing on May 27, 1978, in Woodstock, New York, and they continued through June 8. The Stones then flew to Orlando to rehearse for two more days before the opening show in the Lakeland, Florida, Civic Center. Just under 10,000 attended. The venues on this tour varied from theaters to indoor arenas to outdoor stadiums. Some venues, like JFK Stadium in Philadelphia, were so large that selling out seemed impossible, yet the Stones had over 90,000 fans at the concert there on June 17.

The tour winded its way from Florida to Atlanta; Passaic, New Jersey; Washington, D.C.; Philadelphia; and New York. In Washington, D.C., the Stones played in the smallest venue, the Warner Theater, seating only 2,000. From New York, the tour pushed south again to Hampton Roads, Virginia; Myrtle Beach, South Carolina; Greensboro; Memphis; and Lexington, Kentucky. On July 1 the northern swing began in Cleveland, followed by Buffalo, Detroit, Chicago (at Soldier Field with over 85,000 attending), St. Paul, and St. Louis. Then, after an off day, the band was back south in the Superdome in New Orleans. Two off days followed to get the equipment west and set up in Boulder, Colorado. Then concerts followed in Fort Worth, Houston, Tucson, Anaheim (in Anaheim Stadium), and Oakland. The band did only one show a day and only appeared in one venue (Anaheim) twice. The tour was relatively short (46 days), with 25 shows before almost 800,000 total attendees. It went from June 10 to July 26.

The Peter Tosh Band played as the opening act at all venues, and Etta James appeared at seven performances. Other entertainers who played at least one of the concerts included Patti Smith, Foreigner, Eddie Money, Kansas, April Wine, Van Halen, the Doobie Brothers, and Santana. Reviews were universally positive, emphasizing that the Stones were still relevant and hot. Reviewers praised the amazing energy of the Stones after so many years and performances. It was very satisfying to the band and, as usual, fun but exhausting. Everyone survived the tour, and Keith seemed to be handling his first tour since his heroin withdrawal very well, though his cure was to rely on marijuana and alcohol, mostly the latter.

In late August 1978 the band got together again in Los Angeles to begin recording a new album. Ian Stewart and a couple other studio musicians joined them, and the sessions went on for two weeks. Just as they finished, the band received word that Keith Moon, the drummer for the Who, had died on September 7 in London of a drug overdose. Moon had been close to all the Stones, and Bill and Charlie departed for his funeral, which had to give Keith Richards pause to think about his recent treatment for drug addiction. After the funeral Keith flew to Toronto, where he appeared in court and where his plea bargain was accepted. He was given one year probation and agreed to play a benefit concert for the blind. (As noted earlier, two were actually held on April 22, 1979.)

In January 1979 the band reconvened to record some more, this time in Nassau, Bahamas, favored because of the political instability of Jamaica. The sessions did not go well, and most of the band members left by February 12. In April the whole band convened to do Keith's penance in Oshawa by playing the concert he had agreed to give. The New Barbarians (Keith and Woody's six-member band) played an hour, followed by the Stones. The concerts were hosted by John Belushi, a comedian and movie star, who, ironically, died three years later as a result of a drug overdose. After the concerts, the New Barbarians went on tour for a month in North America.

Mick Jagger was a bit hurt that Keith had formed this band with Ronnie Wood, unbeknownst to Mick. Of course, Mick was now doing solo appearances at times, but he still felt a bit bothered by Keith's actions. Bill Wyman had made a number of solo records by this time, so most of the Stones had other interests that they addressed beyond the band. Charlie's interests were more in Civil War military memorabilia and other collectible objects of art. His wife is a sculptor, so this was an area of mutual interest for them. He continued to see being a Stone as a job and spent as much time with his wife and daughter as possible.

In late May 1979 the Stones released a compilation album in the United Kingdom, *Time Waits for No One*. It had 10 songs from recent albums and was their 10th compilation, though Allan Klein and his ABKCO records had done at least three. This was the third from Rolling Stones Records.

From late June through August 1979, the band was in recording sessions in Paris. Various ailments and arguments led to a lot of wasted time, and little of great quality was produced. In mid-August the New Barbarians played at Knebworth Park with Led Zeppelin (the latter band's last performance, as it turned out), but Woody and Keith returned a couple weeks later to finish the Stones' recording sessions in Paris. After more time off, the band reconvened in Paris in mid-September and worked on recordings through mid-October. Then, in November, Keith and Mick (the Glimmer Twins) met to do the album mixing but had a series of arguments and both left. Also in November, Iranian students took over the U.S. embassy in Teheran and held 52 American hostages. They would not be released until January 1981.

In early December 1979, the Stones got together at a studio in New York, settled their differences, and finished mixing the album.

In early March 1980, Ronnie Wood and his wife, Jo, were arrested for possessing 200 grams of cocaine while vacationing in St. Maarten. After a short stint in jail, they were deported to the United States. Ronnie and Keith were now best buds, as Mick and Keith had a number of differences that led to their less cordial relationship, but Keith and Ronnie seemed to be bad influences on each other. Ronnie's drug and alcohol use was increasing, and Keith was part of that. His drug use had diminished, but his alcohol consumption matched at times that of Ronnie Wood, a considerable feat.

Charlie and Bill met with Keith and Mick in New York in late March to discuss the mixes of the new album (*Emotional Rescue*), and the meeting deteriorated into a shouting match. Some of the tracks were great, while others were not, and the discussion focused on that. More work was to be done as well as publicity photo shoots while they were in New York. Changes were made to the album in March, then again in May, with songs being dropped. Ten songs were kept, with other cuts meant for the next album (which became *Tattoo You*).

In June the order of songs was changed and a single, "Emotional Rescue," was released in both the United States (June 23) and the United Kingdom (June 20). The song rose to number 3 in the United States (19 weeks on the chart) and number 9 in the United Kingdom (8 weeks of listing). The album, also called *Emotional Rescue*, was released in the United States at the same time as the single and a week later in the United Kingdom. The album became number 1 in both the United States (20 weeks on the charts) and the United Kingdom (18 weeks), the first number 1 album in the United Kingdom for the Stones in seven years (since *Goats Head Soup*).

Keith wanted to tour that summer or fall and promote the new album. Mick was noncommittal until he went on vacation to Morocco with Jerry Hall. Then he sent a Telex to the Stones' offices saying that there would be no 1980 tour. Keith was angry, both at Mick's decision and that he had made the decision without talking to Keith face-to-face.

In September the Stones released another single, "She's So Cold," from the new album, and it did well though never made the Top 10 in records for any week. In November Mick and Bianca's divorce was finalized, with a settlement of $1.5 million going to Bianca (later altered to $2.5 million the next year). Mick was mostly in Paris that month working on a new compilation album, *Sucking in the*

Seventies, which included 10 Stones hits from 1974 to 1979. Charlie and Ronnie Wood stopped by to assist a couple times. The album was released in April 1981 and reached number 15 in the United States but failed to chart in the United Kingdom.

On December 8 the Stones and the rest of the world were shocked to hear that late that night, John Lennon had been shot and killed on the street outside his residence, the Dakota, in New York City. John had been close to all the Stones, and for a time he and Mick had been neighbors and frequent visitors to each other's homes in New York. This was mostly when Lennon was living with May Pang. When John and Yoko Ono reconciled, she seemed to screen out most of John's old friends. Nevertheless, the closeness that the Stones felt toward John Lennon was very deep, and there was a great sense of loss at his senseless death. The death shook Mick most of all because of rumors for years that he was a target of various groups or individuals. He became even more wary and traveled with a bodyguard almost everywhere.

In January 1981 the rift between Keith and Mick continued to widen, and there were fears among the other band members that their differences were too great ever to be repaired. Nevertheless, there was talk among the Stones' business entourage of a tour in the summer. If that were to come about, it might be a farewell tour. Woody, Bill, and Keith had all pursued solo albums or work with another band. Mick was still acting in films. Charlie had played drums on Ronnie's solo LP. Even if the band were to break up, all the Stones had careers that they would still pursue.

In late March Mick and Keith met in New York at the Stones' office there and seemed to have a reconciliation that resulted in an agreement to tour in summer or fall 1981, most likely in the United States. The Stones had not toured in three years, not since the U.S. tour of June–July 1978. In April, two new songs were recorded for the upcoming album, which consisted of songs from sessions as far back as the *Goats Head Soup* sessions in 1972. Some had been recorded in Rotterdam in 1975 and others in Paris at the various sessions there over the past three years.

Efforts were made to continue recording in New York in May and June, but Keith did not show up at any of the scheduled sessions, and talk among Charlie, Bill, and Mick returned to considering the dissolution of the band. The guys dispersed but decided to reassemble in late June in New York, where they shot some music videos. They agreed to a tour if Woody would cut down on his drinking and cocaine use and be ready to play regularly at rehearsals and per-formances. With that assurance they scheduled rehearsals for the tour and offered Woody $500,000 if he'd be ready to play on the tour at each venue. Since Wood was still a salaried employee of the Stones, this would be a huge bonus for him.

Rehearsals began in July but were interrupted by Woody's poor preparation, Keith not showing up some nights, and Charlie talk-ing about quitting the band. After 10 days they ended rehearsals, just about the time that the new album, *Tattoo You,* came out (August 18 in the United States and August 28 in the United Kingdom). The album went to number 1 in the United States and was on the charts for 30 weeks, while in the United Kingdom, it hit number 2 and was on the charts for 29 weeks. Hits such as "Start Me Up," "Waiting on a Friend," and "Hang Fire" fed the great popularity of the album.

In mid-August the group reconvened at Longview Farm, in Massachusetts, for another go at rehearsals. The results were as bad as they had been earlier. Keith and Woody were often too out of it to play well, Charlie wasn't sleeping at night and his playing was erratic: the group tried out a few keyboard players before finally feeling com-fortable with Ian McLagan, who'd played with the Stones on the North American tour in 1978.

The band made an undercover appearance (as Blue Sunday and the Cockroaches) at a small club called Sir Morgan's Cave in Worcester, Massachusetts, on September 14, where things went fairly well, but then Mick got sick and they had to cancel another secret appearance in Boston before leaving Longview Farm on September 24, 1981. The tour would begin the next day.

The American Tour of fall 1981 was nearly three whole months and consisted of 50 shows in 28 cities before more than 2 million people. Most of the venues were stadiums with space for more than 50,000; there were a few smaller venues of 5,000 to 15,000 thousand. Demand was so high for tickets that 3.5 million people bid for the 100,000 available seats for the New York concerts. Tickets with a face value of $15 were selling for more than $250 on the black mar-ket. (There were no Internet sites to allow for bids, like Stub Hub, at that time.) Seven of the 11 songs from *Tattoo You* were on the regu-lar playlist for the tour. As had been the pattern, the great success of the new album fed ticket sales and vice versa. Tour gross exceeded $36 million. Besides Ian McLagan, Ian Stewart was the regular piano player. A number of bands played as warm-up to the Stones. Most frequent was George Thorogood and the Destroyers, but other bands/acts that appeared on the tour at least once included the J. Geils Band, Journey, Heart, Van Halen, Stray Cats, the Neville Brothers, Etta James, Tina Turner, ZZ Top, Iggy Pop, Santana, Screaming Jay Hawkins, and Prince. Prince opened in the Los Angeles Coliseum in October, having been discovered by Charlie. He was initially booed by the crowd because of his unusual attire, but his performance soon had them cheering.

The tour began in Philadelphia and traveled to Buffalo; Rockford, Illinois; Boulder; San Diego; Los Angeles; Seattle; and San Francisco before the band had a week off. On October 24, they played in Orlando and then went on to Atlanta; Houston; Dallas; Louisville; East Rutherford, New Jersey; and Hartford before playing two shows at Madison Square Garden in New York on November 12 and 13. After a couple days off in the city, the shows continued in Cleveland, followed by St. Louis; Cedar Falls, Iowa; St. Paul; Chicago (three shows); Syracuse; and the Silverdome in Pontiac, Michigan, on November 30 and December 1. After one of the Chicago shows, the Stones went to the Checkerboard Lounge and sat in with Muddy Waters and his band. The videotape of that evening shows the pride that Waters had in the Stones and the affection that they had for him. Three more days off led to a performance in New Orleans, then three shows in Washington, D.C., and shows in Lexington, Phoenix, Kansas City, and Hampton Roads, Virginia, on December 18 and 19.

Throughout the tour, Keith stayed reasonably alert and ready to play, although there were difficult moments with Ron Wood. Nevertheless, the tour was a great success. The three months also led to a number of arguments among the Stones. As soon as the tour ended, the band split up for various locations, looking forward to at least four months of relaxation before the beginning of their European tour set for late spring 1982.

During the interim the members split for various locations: Bill and Astrid were in Australia and the Far East; Mick was pushing his nascent film career as well as clubbing in New York and Paris while remixing a solo album; Charlie was home with his various collections; and Ron Wood was drinking too much and pursuing his painting.

In early May 1982 the band began rehearsals in England for the European Tour (their first on the Continent in six years), which would have a playlist similar to the American Tour playlist. The tour began on May 26 in Scotland with shows in Aberdeen, Glasgow, and Edinburgh, then a club show in London. After a day off, there were three stadium shows in Rotterdam, Holland, and two more in Hanover,

West Germany. The next day there was a gig in West Berlin, followed by two days off. The tour continued with a show in the Olympic Stadium in Munich, then two shows in Paris and another in Lyon.

Three days later, the tour was in Gothenburg, Sweden, for performances on June 19 and 20. Then there were two more off days before playing in St. James Park in Newcastle-upon-Tyne, followed by two enormous shows at Wembley Stadium in London and a show in Bristol. Two days later they were back in West Germany with three shows in three days in Frankfort, a performance in Vienna, and another in Cologne. In the next week (July 7–13), there were two performances in Madrid and two more in Turin before the tour moved to Zurich, Switzerland, then back to Italy for a show in Naples and one performance in Nice, France, near where the band had lived in the 1970s.

After three days off for relaxation (and to get the massive stage and equipment transported), the Stones closed the tour in Dublin, Ireland, on July 24 and Leeds, United Kingdom, on July 25. In 60 days they did 35 performances in 23 cities in 10 countries, playing before more than 1.6 million fans. Each Stone made about $500,000 from the tour, money much needed by the more profligate spenders like Ronnie Wood, who was still on salary.

In November the band got together for recording sessions in Paris and then celebrated Keith's 39th birthday on December 18, 1982, in St. Denis, just as they finished the recording sessions. They then split up again, Mick and Jerry Hall to Mustique in the Caribbean, where Mick had built a large home near that of Princess Margaret; Charlie and Bill back to England; and Keith and Patti Hansen, whom he had met in 1979 and was soon to marry, back to a home in New York. Ronnie and Jo Karslake, whom he had been with since his divorce from Krissy Wood in 1978, also returned to New York, where they lived not far from Keith and Patti. Bill and Astrid Lundstrom split up after 14 years in spring 1983.

The band regrouped in late January in Paris to finish recordings for the new album and concluded their work in mid-March. In July 1983, Mick turned 40, and the band got together in August in Paris to sign a new recording contract with CBS Records (which was CBS/Sony in Japan and became wholly owned by Sony in 1987). The contract was reportedly worth more than $50 million, the biggest record deal in history.

Their continued popularity, based on the recent tours, was obvious. The band had continued to stay together, play well together, and attract enormous crowds, while pumping out great records. How long could it continue? Bill was almost 50, and the others were 40, except for Ronnie, who was 36. How long could this go on? The remainder of the 1980s would be a turning point in the band's existence that would address these questions.

NOTES

1. Though AIDS would not be named as such until 1981, it was identified as early as 1978 in the United States and Sweden.
2. Robert Palmer (1983), *The Rolling Stones,* Garden City, NY: Doubleday, p. 211.
3. See Kris Needs (2004), *Keith Richards: Before They Make Me Run,* London: Plexus, chap. 9, and Tony Sanchez (1979), *Up and Down with the Rolling Stones,* New York: William Morrow, chap. 30.
4. Ronnie Wood (2007), *Ronnie: The Autobiography,* New York: St. Martin's Griffin, p. 144, says that they were "great pals." Christopher Andersen (1993), *Jagger, Unauthorized,* New York: Delacorte Press, p. 328, implies that there were affairs with both Jagger and Wood.
5. Bill Wyman, with Richard Havers (2002), *Rolling with the Stones,* London: DK, p. 444.
6. See Needs, *Keith Richards,* p. 201; Stephen Davis (2001), *Old Gods Almost Dead: The 40-Year Odyssey of the Rolling Stones,* New York: Broadway Books, p. 438; Wood, *Ronnie,* p. 188.

CHAPTER SEVEN

Individual Efforts:
Are the Stones Through?

November 1983 saw the release of the album *Undercover*, which the Stones had worked on beginning in the prior November 1982 and continuing through various sessions in Paris at Pathe Marconi Studio and in New York at the Hit Factory. The album had 10 songs, and they were entirely new, their first totally new album of the 1980s. It also followed a video called "Let's Spend the Night Together" that had been released in 1982 and filmed from the 1981 concert tour of the United States. This was an attempt to adjust to the new MTV format that rock music was beginning to adopt.

The album was an immediate hit, rising to number 3 in the United Kingdom and number 4 in the United States but not producing any big singles hits. "Undercover of the Night" did get into the Top 10 in both the United Kingdom and the United States, but that was it for singles' success. Keith and Mick added Chris Kimsey, a sound engineer, as a third producer, which may have reflected their work on other projects at times or, more likely, the continuing gulf that was forming in their personal and professional relationship.

Earlier that fall, Charlie and Bill had been asked to be part of a series of charity concerts to raise money for (and awareness of) multiple sclerosis research. Those concerts began in London's Royal Albert Hall and included Eric Clapton, Steve Winwood, Jimmy

Page, Jeff Beck, and other rock notables. The concerts were reprised in late November in the United States with shows in Dallas, Los Angeles, San Francisco, and New York. Ron Wood joined them for the New York show, and Joe Cocker played the shows in the United States also. In December Keith and Patti Hansen were married on Keith's 40th birthday in Cabo San Lucas, Mexico, with Mick as best man. This was a surprise to some because of their bickering, but they were still the oldest of friends, just friends who wanted to punch out the other at times.

There had been discussions in the fall about a tour of the Far East and Japan in spring 1984 and an American Tour in the summer, but there was too much tension among the band to make any of this happen. Woody's drinking and drug use were beginning to affect his performances and irritate the others, especially Mick, because of Ron's unreliability. Keith and Mick were having problems dealing with each other. Mick was recording a solo album (*She's the Boss*), which was subsequently released in 1985. Keith was upset that Mick was doing a solo album and also upset that in the recording sessions in May 1984, Jeff Beck, Pete Townshend, Herbie Hancock, and Carlos Alomar were involved but Keith was not asked to be a part. Ronnie Wood had done a solo album after officially joining the Stones, but all the Stones had played on it. (This was *Gimme Some Neck*, 1979.) His 1981 album, *1234*, had Charlie on it, but Keith and Mick were busy with other projects. So there were continuing, festering tensions between Keith and Mick.

It was around this time that Charlie Watts began drinking more heavily and using heroin. He was seen as the quieter Stone, and because of his continued faithfulness to his wife, there was also a belief that he was not involved with abusive substances. But he suffered bouts of insomnia on the tours, largely because of not sleeping with his wife, and he turned more and more to drink and heroin during the period beginning about 1983. It was not until some time in 1986 that he was able to defeat his inner demons and control his drinking while ceasing the use of heroin. His wife, Shirley, threatened to leave him, and he finally managed to come to grips with the problems.

Mick and Keith worked once again with Chris Kimsey to produce the compilation album *Rewind (1971–1984)*, which was released in late June 1984. It was issued in both a U.K. and U.S. form and repeated a number of songs from *Sucking in the Seventies*, so it was not nearly the success that the latter had been. It was the last Stones album for Atlantic.

After a meeting in Paris in June 1984, the four original Stones agreed to put aside their differences enough to try recording a new album. There was an attempted get-together in Amsterdam in October 1984. In an effort at amity, Keith took Mick out for a drink, and they came back in the early hours of the morning. Both were quite drunk, and Mick called Charlie's hotel room, where he had finally gotten to sleep after his usual insomnia. Mick's phone call awakened him, but what Mick said aroused him: "Is this my drummer? Why don't you get your arse down here?" was his response to Charlie's lifting the phone. Charlie replaced the phone in the cradle, showered, shaved, and dressed in a Savile Row suit. (He has been named a Best Dressed Man by some publications.) He then came to Mick's room and punched him into a bowl of smoked salmon, according to Ronnie Wood.[1] Charlie then lifted Mick up and was about to punch him out the window, but Mick was saved from toppling 20 stories into a canal by Keith grabbing Mick's legs. Charlie then told Mick, "Don't ever call me 'your drummer' again. You're my f—ing singer." This was Charlie's way of reminding Mick that he shouldn't disrespect him. It also illustrated the stress that Charlie was under with his insomnia and alcohol use.

Another attempt at recording came in January 1985 in Paris. These sessions in Paris were very slow and often very unproductive. The tension between Mick and Keith was palpable, and Mick often walked out early to work on his solo album. Keith, then, was leading the band, and the tension was eased. It also allowed for Ronnie to do some of the writing and arranging. Recording sessions went on sporadically through June, then again from mid-July into October. It was far more tedious than any album work had been, and the result was the first album in years in which the songs were not all by Keith and Mick. Four of the cuts on *Dirty Work* were also credited to Ronnie Wood (as well as Keith and Mick), and two, "Too Rude" and "Harlem Shuffle," were covers. Keith sings lead on two cuts, a new development for the band. Charlie was not drumming on a number of songs, and guest drummers (including Ron Wood on "Sleep Tonight") were necessary to overcome Charlie's debilitation due to his addictions. The album, released in March 1986 in both the United Kingdom and the United States, reached number 4 in both charts, remaining on them for 10 weeks in the United Kingdom and 15 in the United States.

In July 1985, when the rehearsals were on hiatus, Bob Dylan dropped in on Ronnie Wood at his home in New York City. Dylan asked Wood to do a charity gig with him, and Woody agreed. Then Keith happened to call Ronnie on the phone while Dylan was there, and Wood asked Dylan if Keith could be a part of the gig, too. Dylan was enthusiastic, Richards came by from his New York home nearby, and the three began rehearsing Dylan songs. Neither of the Stones seemed aware of the nature of the gig, but on July 13, 1985, the limo that was sent to pick them up headed to Philadelphia, where they were part of what was the biggest concert ever broadcast, Live Aid for Africa, with simultaneous broadcasts in Philadelphia's JFK Stadium and London's Wembley Stadium. There were 99,000 and 82,000 at the two sites, respectively, and another 400 million heard or saw the broadcast in 60 countries. Dylan, Wood, and Richards sang two Dylan songs near the end of the 14-hour concert. Just prior to their singing, Mick sang with Hall and Oates, Eddie Kendrick, and David Ruffin as well as with Tina Turner.

Following completion of the *Dirty Work* album in New York, in fall 1985, discussion ensued about a tour to promote the album, but Mick refused to agree to promote the album and went on tour to promote his second solo album, *Primitive Cool*. This made band tension even worse and essentially shut down the Stones as an enterprise, at least temporarily.

In December the Stones were all shocked and distraught over the sudden death of Ian Stewart, a cofounder of the group who had continued to play for recording sessions, manage their road locations, and keep the band members humbler with his Scottish wit and repartee. Stewart died of heart failure on December 12 at the age of 47. Ian's death was an even bigger blow than that of Brian Jones since Ian was not a drug user and kept a reasonably healthy life (other than fatty foods). Also he was the moral compass of the band and had known them all since the inception of the Rolling Stones. He could call them on poor performances, and his suggestions were always heeded. Ian was trusted and loved by all the Stones, and his loss left a gaping hole in all their hearts. All the band plus many others in music in England, such as Eric Clapton and Jeff Beck, attended his funeral. A memorial show was held in February 1986 at the 100 Club in London with lots of musicians sitting in with Ian's band, Rocket 88. All the Stones were there, as were Pete Townshend, Eric Clapton, Jeff Beck, Jack Bruce, and Simon Kirke. It was a celebration of Ian's life, closed by a short clip of him playing "Key to the Highway," recorded during the *Dirty Work* sessions. *Dirty Work* was released in late March to generally unfavorable reviews, despite excellent sales.

In early March the Stones were honored with a Grammy for Lifetime Achievement. The award was presented in London by Eric Clapton. Interestingly, the Stones had never won a Grammy before, so this was a long overdue honor.

The summer was filled with individual projects since the band was not going to tour. Most were working on individual albums or with other people on albums. Charlie put together a big band, a 35-piece jazz orchestra, and they played a bit as well as making a recording. Keith was working on a documentary film on Chuck Berry, and Keith played and sang vocals on it. Also playing were Chuck Leavell and Bobby Keys, regular Stones studio and touring musicians, and Steve Jordan from Keith's solo band. Ronnie and his wife, Jo, went to New Orleans in June to tape an HBO concert special, and Ronnie got to play with Fats Domino, Jerry lee Lewis, and Ray Charles. Keith had been the inducter when Berry was the first inductee into the Rock and Roll Hall of Fame in January 1986. Mick was promoting his second solo album. Bill celebrated his 50th birthday on October 24. Though he felt great, his birthday made the question of longevity as a rock musician very appropriate. Bill had been the band archivist in keeping records of everything that the band had ever done, and he decided to pursue the notion of an autobiography. Four years later, it became a reality when *Stone Alone*, coauthored with Ray Coleman, was published.

The year 1987 was again a year of mostly independent projects: Charlie's orchestra, Ron Wood's painting (after doing a tour with Bo Diddley the year before), Keith's solo album, Mick's continued solo work, and Bill's work trying to develop young bands. The five hardly saw each other, though they all did get together at Keith's 44th birthday party on July 26, 1987. The Stones were not news for that year, and the persistent rumors of their demise as a group resurfaced.

On January 20, 1988, the Beatles were inducted into the Rock and Roll Hall of Fame, and Mick was the presenter. The previous year Keith had been the presenter for Aretha Franklin. Mick called Bill Wyman just before the induction of the Beatles and asked how Bill felt about touring. Mick and Keith were still feuding, but Mick was considering a tour so things might get reconciled.

Nevertheless, 1988 was a continued year of individual projects for the Stones. Woody continued his touring with Bo Diddley, and Keith did some recording in Memphis, Bermuda, and Montserrat. Mick did a tour of Japan. Bill continued his work promoting young bands and got a number of musicians to play a show supporting his project. It was held at the Albert Hall and featured Phil Collins, Simon Kirke, Chrissie Hynde, and Jeff Beck, among others.

In mid-May 1988, the band met in London at the Savoy Hotel with their financial manager, Prince Rupert Lowenstein, who had finally gotten all their debts, contracts, and obligations in order. It was clear that individual projects would preclude any organized tour or recording by the Stones for the rest of 1988. The question was, would there be any after that? The question was not settled, though there remained the possibility of recording in early 1989 and touring after that as part of the album's release/promotion. The differences between Keith and Mick were still evident.

Later in the year, Woody claimed that he got the two of them to talk on the phone together and resolve their differences, which both thought were based on exaggerations in the press and their individual stubbornness.[2] In August Keith and Mick met briefly in New York, but both were about to embark on solo tours. Mick went to Australia, Indonesia, and New Zealand. Keith toured in the United States with his X-Pensive Winos band. Shortly after Keith's tour ended (in late December 1988), he met with Mick in Barbados in mid-January 1989, where they agreed that they wanted to work together again and began working on material for a new album.

The timing for the Stones' reconciliation was perfect as they were being inducted into the Rock and Roll Hall of Fame on January 16, 1989, along with Dion, Otis Redding, Stevie Wonder, and the Temptations. Charlie and Bill didn't attend, but Mick Taylor joined Mick, Keith, and Ron Wood at the ceremony in New York. Pete Townshend introduced the Stones, admonishing them not to grow old gracefully since "it wouldn't suit you." Mick was the spokesperson, and he paid tribute to Brian Jones and Ian Stewart as band founders, members, and dear friends. Things had turned around for Mick and Keith, and the Stones all gathered the next month in Barbados to begin rehearsing for a new album. After two weeks, the band took a break then reconvened in Montserrat to start recording at Air Studios.

A new distraction arose at this time when Mandy Smith, whom Bill had been dating since breaking up with Astrid, leaked to the press the information that she and Bill were to be married. This was intriguing to many because Bill had begun dating Mandy when she was 13 and he 47. Mandy's mother initially chaperoned their dates. That had been in 1983. Now they were to be engaged when she was 18 and he 52. Bill flew to Antigua to meet with the press for a couple days, then returned to Montserrat on April 3 to continue recording.

Recording sessions went through May 2, at which time Bill returned to London to organize his wedding set for June 2. Despite the circus atmosphere, all the Stones and their wives attended the wedding in London. During that month, the Stones also began mixing the new album (*Steel Wheels*) at Olympic Studios in London, where they had recorded their first six albums in the 1960s and 1970s. The album was to be promoted by the biggest tour that the Stones had ever done, possibly the biggest ever done, the Steel Wheels Tour, which, in its second year, was then referred to as the Urban Jungle Tour. The tour was announced on July 11 in New York's Grand Central Station. The Stones had not toured the United States in eight years and had not toured at all in seven, so this was seen as a kind of rebirth of the band. Whether they would draw as well and whether they would perform as well as in the past remained to be seen.

Directly after the press conference in New York, the Stones headed to Southbury, Connecticut, to begin rehearsing for the tour at a girl's school that had recently closed. Six weeks later, a warm-up show was done at a small club (seating 700) in New Haven called Toad's Place on August 12, 1989. The band then went to Long Island, where they rehearsed for two more weeks in the Nassau Coliseum on the Steel Wheels stage. The stage was massive and the sets were designed by stage designer Mark Fisher, based on the vision and input of Charlie and Mick. The whole construction took 80 trucks to haul it from city to city and a crew of 200 to rebuild it at each venue, with the assistance of 150 locals.

The album *Steel Wheels* was released on August 29, just two days before the tour began. It immediately was a best seller, rising to number 3 in the United States and number 2 in the United Kingdom, and received rave reviews, though its heavy disco influence seems dated now. Most of the reviews commented on the desultory albums that had immediately preceded, that is, *Dirty Work* and *Undercover*. It was noted that the Stones were fabulous once again. There were great singles on the album, most notably "Mixed Emotions," a confessional of sorts by Mick regarding his relationship with Keith. That song, released as a single, hit number 1 and number 5 in various charts. Other top singles from the album were "Almost Hear You Sigh," "Rock and a Hard Place," and "Terrifying," all of which made it into the Top 10 in one of the charts. "Continental Drift" was both a paean to Brian Jones and an illustration of the world music quality that the Stones had taken on. This song was accompanied by the Master Musicians of Jajouka, Morocco, the same pipe musicians with whom Brian had recorded in 1969. The recording had been done in Tangier, Morocco, after which the Stones had flown back to London.

The tour was promoted by a Canadian, Michael Cohl, who guaranteed the Stones $70 million, far more than Bill Graham had promised. Thus the Stones went on a North American tour not sponsored by Graham for the first time in at least 15 years, and Graham was shocked and disoriented by the loss of the Stones. The North American tour would run 112 days, nearly four months, and would surely tax everyone's energy in the band and the support crew. Each show was two hours, and tickets were $30 or more face value, much higher in resale. The tour program cost $14. The band's gross for the five months (including rehearsals) was about $200 million. In the 112 days, there were 61 shows in 36 venues in the United States and Canada.

The playlist was a mix of old and new, with only three songs from the new album. Opening acts were either Living Colour or Guns N' Roses. The band that accompanied the Stones had seven pieces with regulars Chuck Leavell, Bobby Keys, and Matt Clifford joined by four other horns and three backing vocalists. Reviews of the tour were universally positive.

The tour began in Philadelphia's Veterans Stadium before 55,000 on August 31 and September 1. After a day for travel, there were two shows in Toronto's Exhibition Stadium, then a show in Pittsburgh's Three Rivers Stadium. There followed three shows at Alpine Valley Resort in East Troy, Wisconsin, about 15 miles north of Illinois and 75 miles north of Chicago. Three days later the tour was in another baseball stadium, Riverfront in Cincinnati, for one show, then they were off to Raleigh, St. Louis, and Louisville. On September 21 and 22, the Stones did their first performance of the tour inside, at the Carrier Dome in Syracuse. Then it was back to large outdoor venues: RFK Stadium in Washington, D.C., Municipal Stadium in Cleveland, four shows in Foxboro Stadium in Massachusetts, and a day off before playing in Birmingham, Alabama, at Legion Field.

Another off day allowed for travel to the upper Midwest, where the tour rolled into Ames, Iowa, at Cyclone Stadium, then Arrowhead Stadium in Kansas City. Another day off led to two shows in Shea Stadium in New York. Then the band got a week off before reconvening in Los Angeles at the Coliseum for four shows in five days. They went back to New York three days later for four more performances at Shea. Three days after that they set up in Vancouver,

British Columbia, for two shows, then headed south to Oakland's Alameda Stadium for two more shows. Two days later, there was a show at the Astrodome in Houston, then two shows in Texas Stadium in Dallas, one indoors at the Superdome in New Orleans, and another two at the Orange Bowl in Miami.

This schedule was a real endurance test for all; the next stop was Tampa on November 18. Two days later they were in Atlanta before three days off. After this short rest they reconvened at the Gator Bowl in Jacksonville, then moved on to Clemson, South Carolina, before having two days off to allow the stage to get to Minneapolis. There were two shows at the Metrodome, then two more off days before playing SkyDome in Toronto, which had been occupied with baseball when the Stones had been there in September. The final venues were all indoors as the weather had now grown cold. These were the Hoosier Dome in Indianapolis, the Silverdome in Detroit, the Olympic Stadium in Montreal, and the Convention Center in Atlantic City, where the Stones closed with three shows on December 17, 19, and 20. In all more than three million people attended shows on the tour. One nice part of the tour was that all the wives and some of the Stones' children traveled with much of the tour, except for Mandy Smith Wyman, who remained in England and had some health issues.

The grueling tour had made Christmas in 1989 even more welcome than usual, especially since the band was going to continue the tour in the Pacific beginning in February. This section of the tour was relatively short: two weeks, 10 shows, all in Tokyo's Korakuen Dome, which had opened in 1988. More than 500,000 attended the 10 shows, bringing in a gross of about $30 million. The tour ran from February 14 to 27, and the Stones returned home to rest up and rehearse for the European leg of the tour, which would begin in May.

The group began rehearsing in early May northwest of Paris at the Chateau de Dangu before opening the new tour in Rotterdam on May 18 before 47,000 spectators. This version of the tour was now to be called the Urban Jungle Tour, but the playlist was essentially the same as in Steel Wheels, though a few songs shorter. Besides the generally shorter playlist, there was a new stage set designed by Mark Fisher and Jonathan Park, which cost $40 million. The stage was 236 feet wide and the set 82 feet high. Each night at the finale, fireworks costing almost $50,000 were set off. It was an amazing performance each night, and almost 2.5 million got to witness the 46 shows during the 100 days of the tour.

As in Steel Wheels, almost all the venues were outdoor stadiums, though smaller than the American stadiums, but for Wembley. After three shows in Rotterdam, the tour played nine shows in the newly united Germany over a period of two weeks. These were in Hannover, Frankfurt, Cologne, Munich, and Berlin. From there they set off for Iberia to play their first show in Lisbon, then shows in Barcelona and Madrid. They went on to France with a performance in Marseilles, then three in Paris, followed by a show in Basel, Switzerland. There were six days off before three shows in Wembley Stadium in London. This meant that the Stones were basically home for about 10 days in the middle of the tour, and it was a needed respite.

From London, the tour went north to Glasgow on July 9 before another week off. They began again on July 16 in Cardiff, Wales, and went to Newcastle-upon-Tyne and Manchester before departing the United Kingdom once again on July 22. The next stops were Rome for three shows, Turin, and Vienna. After another two-day break for travel, the tour relocated in Gothenburg, Sweden, for two shows, Oslo for two more, and Copenhagen. On August 13 and 14, the band played in the former East Berlin, then in Gelsenkirchen, Germany, and did a show in Prague on August 18, their first visit to Czechoslovakia (which split peacefully into the Czech Republic and Slovakia in 1993). This last concert was played before 110,000 people, including the Czech president, Vaclav Havel. The Stones took another week to get back to London, where they played their final two concerts in Wembley once again on August 24 and 25.

These two concerts would be the last that Bill Wyman would play as a Rolling Stone. Bill's father had died during the tour to Japan. His marriage had been limited to very few days because of the nearly year-long tour. Mandy's health had not been good when he was home. Bill was to be 54 in October. He had become very concerned about plane crashes. Ronnie Wood noted that on the Steel Wheels Tour, Bill kept saying that this would be his last tour, that he was quitting the band once they were finally home. No one really believed him, however, despite Bill's growing disturbance at flying. They figured that when the next tour came up in another year or so, he'd put aside his flying problems and go back on tour. They were wrong on two counts. The next tour wasn't for four years (August 1994), and Bill was long gone as a Stone by then.

In addition to his departure from the Stones (which did not actually occur until January 1993), Bill also was divorced from his wife, Mandy, in 1991. It had been, in his words, "a disaster from the word go,"[3] as many had predicted it would be. He reconnected with his American girlfriend from 1979, Suzanne Accosta, and they were married on April 21, 1993.

The tour ended in late August 1990, and the band members went their own ways once again. Mick promoted his second album and began work on a third. Jerry Hall issued an ultimatum that he marry her or they would have to split up. Mick insisted on a prenuptial agreement to protect his fortune. Jerry's modeling had made her a multimillionaire also, so she agreed to one.[4] With that, they were finally married, after 12 years together, in Bali on November 21, 1990. Keith worked on his own album, recording with blues legend John Lee Hooker. Mick costarred in the movie *Freejack*. Charlie recorded with his orchestra. Ron Wood returned to his home in Ireland.

The band did get together in January 1991 to record a few new tracks, and two of them, "Highwire" and "Sex Drive," were placed on a new live album, *Flashpoint*, which was drawn from the Steel Wheels/Urban Jungle tours of 1989–1990. That album was released in April 1991 and sold reasonably well. "Highwire," which was a commentary on the first Gulf War, was released as a single and rose to number 6 in the United Kingdom and number 16 in the United States.

In November 1991, the Stones signed a new record contract with Virgin Records for $45 million. The Stones agreed to produce three albums and to sell the rights to their albums back to 1971 and *Sticky Fingers*. Mick recorded his only solo album of the 1990s, *Wandering Spirit*, for Atlantic from January to September 1992. It was released in February 1993 and was quite successful, rising to number 12 in the United Kingdom and number 11 in the United States, remaining on the charts for 16 weeks and becoming a gold album.

In November 1992 Charlie and Mick visited Bill and asked him to reconsider his decision to leave the band, which had now been rumored but not officially acknowledged. Bill said he was happy with what he was doing and would make the official announcement of his departure soon. That occurred on a television show, *London Tonight*, in January 1993.

In May 1992 Mick's daughter by Marsha Hunt, Karis, graduated from Yale, and Mick and Jerry attended the graduation. Then in July, Mick's daughter Jade gave birth to a baby girl. Mick, just short of his 49th birthday, was a grandfather, just a few months after Jerry Hall had given birth to Mick's daughter, Georgia May, on January 12.

He now had five children: one with Marsha Hunt, one with Bianca, and three with Jerry.

In November 1992 Keith and his X-Pensive Winos band went on tour to promote their album *Main Offender* (released in October 1992). The tour began in Buenos Aries, Argentina, went to the United States and Europe, and finished in February 1993. The last shows were at New York's Beacon Theatre, and all six sold out the 4,000-capacity venue for the shows on February 19–24. Ron Wood's album *Slide on This* was released in September 1992, and he went on tour in the United States and Japan to promote it from late October 1992 to January 1993. Another album, *Slide on Live*, resulted from that tour and was released in late September 1993. Charlie released two albums during this period with his Charlie Watts Quintet. The first was *From One Charlie* (February 1991) and the second was *Tribute to Charlie Parker with Strings* (August 1992). He also did a solo album, *Warm and Tender*, which was released in December 1993.

The Stones had survived the loss of Bill Wyman as they each went off on their own projects. They were now ready to come together once again for what would be another rebirth of the Rolling Stones in 1994.

NOTES

1. Ronnie Wood (2007), *Ronnie: The Autobiography*, New York: St. Martin's Griffin, pp. 242–43. Also recounted by Christopher Andersen (1993), *Jagger, Unauthorized*, New York: Delacorte Press, p. 371.
2. Wood, *Ronnie*, p. 248.
3. Bill Wyman, with Richard Havers (2002), *Rolling with the Stones*, London: DK, p. 496.
4. So claimed Andersen, *Jagger, Unauthorized*, p. 396. Also see Stephen Davis (2001), *Old Gods Almost Dead: The 40-Year Odyssey of the Rolling Stones*, New York: Broadway Books, p. 515.

CHAPTER EIGHT

From *Voodoo Lounge* to *Bridges to Babylon* and Beyond

In early 1993 Mick, Keith, Charlie, and Ronnie reassembled in Barbados at Eddie Grant's Ocean Wave Studios to plan and rehearse the next album and tour. Keith and Mick had done some musical "dabbling" earlier that year in New York, but what they needed, they both agreed, was a focus. They wrote a number of songs, and the band did some initial recording in summer 1993 in Ireland, first at Ron Wood's home and then at Windmill Lane Studios, Dublin. The needed focus would come partially from Charlie and might also come from a new bass player. Keith had been very angry over Bill's departure from the band and actually thought of forcing him to play at gunpoint. Luckily he did not and noted later that he understood Bill's departure and was good with it. Nevertheless, the rhythm section, that is, Bill and Charlie on bass and drums, respectively, had often carried the songs, and it was imperative to get a bassist with whom the band was comfortable personally and professionally.

In June 1993, in New York, the band had recruitment tryouts, as they had for Ronnie Wood, and similarly the bassist they hired, Darryl Jones, was not announced as a new Stone. Ronnie had been hired for the tour in 1975 and did not become an official member of the Stones until 1976. It was not until 1993, however, that he became a full partner in the Stones' contracts. So Darryl Jones, a relatively young African American man of 32, would be the bassist for the new album and tour. He and Charlie got on very well, it seemed, and that was vital since their support of the lead had to be in synch both musically and emotionally.

After recording in Ireland through early December, the band went on hiatus until mid-January 1994, when they reconvened in Los Angeles, where they were mixing until the end of April. During all this, there had been a singular honor announced for Mick and Keith when they were inducted into the Songwriters Hall of Fame in June 1993. Keith accepted the award in New York for the duo and saw it as one of the most satisfying and flattering moments in his career. Another highlight in December was Keith's 50th birthday, which coincided with his 10th wedding anniversary to Patti. There was a party in New York at Metropolis Restaurant with 150 guests, including Eric Clapton, Kate Moss, Bobby Keys, the rest of the Stones, and Keith's family.

Recording for the new album *Voodoo Lounge* (named after a cat that Keith befriended and later adopted in Barbados) went surprisingly smoothly. The mixing by Don Was cleaned up a lot of the proverbial rough edges, and the album was released on July 11, 1994, about a month before the Voodoo Lounge Tour would commence. The album went to number 1 in the United Kingdom and Australia and to number 2 in the United States, and five singles from the album were released and made the Top 100 record charts for either 1994 or 1995. Despite the ballyhoo for *Steel Wheels*, it was an uneven album with rough discordant sounds in places and a heavy, dated disco beat, which was popular at the time. *Voodoo Lounge*, by contrast, though it was released to mixed reviews, does not show its age and can be equated with some of the best of the Stones' albums like *Sticky Fingers, Let It Bleed*, or *Beggars Banquet*.

The top singles in terms of sales were "Love Is Strong" and "You Got Me Rocking." "Sparks Will Fly" is a great rocking song, but its lyrics kept it from being played as widely on mainstream radio. This was also true of "Thru and Thru," with Keith singing lead. Keith's song "The Worst" was a heartfelt and gritty song that typified him and made the song more appealing. Over 4 million copies of the album were sold in 1994 alone. As part of their recordings, the band now regularly made high-quality (and high-cost) videos, which also helped album and record sales.

The almost immediate success of the album boded well for the upcoming tour, which would eventually run even longer and cover more miles than the Steel Wheels/Urban Jungle tours. The Voodoo

Lounge Tour would open in August in Washington, D.C., and the North American section would again be performed mostly in outdoor stadiums with capacities of at least 50,000. The tour was announced on May 4 in New York harbor, aboard a former yacht of John F. Kennedy's that was moored there. Rehearsals began in June and were held in the Toronto area in the gymnasium of a boy's boarding academy, Greenwood Private School.

On July 19 the band played a warm-up session at a small club in Toronto called RPM. The cost was five dollars for the cover, and they were scheduled to start the set at 8:30 P.M. A local musician, Jeff Healey, played an opening set, then the stage was set up with the Stones' gear. The Stones were introduced by Michael Cohl, who was again promoting the tour. For the 1,100 or so fans fortunate enough to get in, the gig was hard-driving and intimate. The Stones were indeed back, and the promise of a highly successful tour was obvious.

The first leg of the North American tour went 140 days and had 60 concerts in 42 cities. The stage was again enormous and required a crew of 250 to assemble and break down at each venue. The stage setting cost $4 million. The playlist for the tour had a mixture of old favorites and six of the songs from the *Voodoo Lounge* album. Tickets were priced at $50 or more, and there were empty seats at some venues.

After two shows in RFK Stadium on August 1 and 3, the tour went to Birmingham, Alabama, for a show, then to Indianapolis to the RCA Dome and on to Giants Stadium in East Rutherford, New Jersey, for four shows in six nights. Two nights later, there were shows on consecutive nights in Toronto at CNE Stadium, then three nights later, a show in Winnipeg. The month of August ended with the band doing shows in Camp Randall Stadium in Madison, Cleveland Stadium, and Riverfront Stadium in Cincinnati.

There were five days before the next concerts, two in Sullivan Stadium in Foxboro, Massachusetts, then single shows in Raleigh and East Lansing, Michigan, before two shows in Chicago's Soldier Field, an enormous stadium on the lakefront. The tour then headed west, where the Stones did a show in Denver's Mile High Stadium, followed by one in Columbia, Missouri. Then there was another shift back East for two shows in Veterans Stadium in Philadelphia, one in Columbia, South Carolina, one in Memphis, and another in Pittsburgh's Three Rivers Stadium to end September.

During that month the Stones were saddened by the death of Nicky Hopkins, the fabulous keyboardist who had played on many of their albums from the late 1960s until 1980. Hopkins had also done some touring with the Stones but had had to curtail that because of his difficulties with Crohn's disease, from which he had suffered since childhood. Ultimately the disease took his life at the age of 50.[1]

October began with the last outdoor concerts in northern climates, in Ames, Iowa, and Commonwealth Stadium in Edmonton, Alberta, Canada, on October 4 and 5. Travel south gave the band a few days off before playing in the Louisiana Superdome on October 10. Four days later they did two shows in Las Vegas for the first time, then went to San Diego and the Rose Bowl in Pasadena for two more shows there. There was a fast trip to Salt Lake City before returning to California to do four shows in six nights in Oakland, the last on Halloween.

The November concerts were all in warm locales beginning with shows in Texas (El Paso, San Antonio, and Houston), with a jaunt to Little Rock between the last two Texas locales. They did two shows in Atlanta and made a return to Texas to play one show in the Cotton Bowl in Dallas. The month ended with Florida shows in Tampa, Miami, and Gainesville, closing on November 27.

Four nights later, the Stones began a series of concerts in large, domed stadiums in northern locations. First there was the Silverdome in Pontiac, Michigan, then SkyDome in Toronto and Olympic Stadium in Montreal for two shows. Syracuse's Carrier Dome was the next venue, followed by the Metrodome in Minneapolis, the Kingdome in Seattle, and finally, two shows in Vancouver's BC Place Stadium. This last show of the U.S./Canada leg was on December 18, Keith's 51st birthday. He was forced to miss his son's wedding in Italy, but some of his disappointment had to be assuaged by the fact that this leg of the tour grossed over $140 million.

The tour took a break from December 19 to January 14 for rest and celebrating the holidays with families. Keith and Ronnie decided to rent a yacht for three weeks to sail around the Caribbean with their families. Charlie went back to England and Mick to Mustique and New York. All reconvened in Mexico City in mid-January, where the Stones did the Voodoo Lounge show four times in a week before 50,000 fans each night, in the baseball stadium located within the Autodromo Hermanos Rodriguez in northeast Mexico City.

Following these shows in Mexico was the beginning of the Stones' first South American tour, something Keith had pushed for since he had played in Argentina a few years previously. The South

American leg of Voodoo Lounge began on January 27 in Sao Paulo, Brazil. In nine days the Stones did five shows at a packed stadium seating 60,000. A week after the Brazilian concerts, on February 9, the Stones began a series of five concerts in eight nights at the River Plate Stadium in Buenos Aires. Three nights later the band did one show in Santiago, Chile, in the National Stadium before departing for South Africa, where they gave two concerts in Johannesburg on February 24 and 25, 1995, their first visit to give a concert on the African continent.

Less than a week later, the band set up in Tokyo, Japan, where they did seven sold-out shows in 12 nights at the Tokyo Dome. Five nights later, the Stones did two shows in two nights in Fukuoka on the Japanese island of Kyushu, about 700 miles southwest of Tokyo. The band also did some recording and remixing at a studio in Japan before heading off to Australia, where they opened in Melbourne on March 27, 1995.

The Voodoo Lounge Tour would be in Australia for 18 days. During that time the Stones played seven shows, in Melbourne (two), Sydney (two), Adelaide (two), and Perth. The Stones had played there before and were wildly popular, and the stadiums were packed. On April 16 and 17, the band did two shows in Auckland, New Zealand, which closed the Pacific leg of the tour.

There would be a gap of nearly two months before the tour resumed in June in Europe. After about a month off, they came together in Holland, first for rehearsals, then for a rehearsal/club performance like they had done in Toronto. The venue was the Paradiso Club in Amsterdam. The Stones played a semiacoustic set to a capacity of 800 for three nights in late May. The shows were recorded and were part of the next live album that the Stones would release the following November 1995.

A week later the Stones began the European leg of the Voodoo Lounge extravaganza by opening in Stockholm's Olympic Stadium on June 3. The band completed the Nordic loop by playing in Helsinki on June 6, Oslo on June 9, and Copenhagen on June 11, before heading back to the Netherlands. There they did two shows in Nijmegen in eastern Holland and one in Landgraaf in the southeast near Belgium and Germany. The tour did only two shows in Germany in June, one in Cologne and one in Hannover, though they would swing back later in the summer to perform in eastern German venues. After Germany, there were two shows in Belgium, at the festival ground in Werchter, about 20 miles northeast of Brussels. Many of the locales were new venues, selected both to appeal to fans who hadn't been able to travel to see them and because the Stones wanted to see other regions and venues, so they pushed for these new sites.

On June 30 and July 1, the tour played at a large racecourse in Paris, then at the Olympia Paris, a music hall, two nights later. This latter performance was recorded and became another part of the live album, which was released the next November. After Paris, the band took almost a week off, most of it spent in and around London, and they returned to the tour on July 9 in Sheffield, about 150 miles north of London. Beginning July 11, the Stones played four performances in London in eight nights, three in Wembley Stadium and one in Brixton Academy in South London. Again the latter performance was recorded to go with the Amsterdam and Paris recordings that would encompass part of the new live album. This set was on July 19 and was played before about 4,000, the capacity of Brixton.

Three nights later the tour was in Gijon, Spain, about 200 miles north of Madrid on the Atlantic coast, where they played in a soccer stadium. Then they went on to Lisbon and then to Montpelier in the south of France. While in Lisbon, the Stones also recorded in the studio for three days. These recordings, plus those made in Tokyo and the live appearances on the tour, would constitute the basis for the new album, which was called *Stripped.* On July 29 and 30 the band played in the soccer stadium of Basel, Switzerland, before appearing in Zeltwag in central Austria. Following an appearance in Munich at the Olympic Stadium, the Stones tour spent about two weeks playing in some cities that had been behind the Iron Curtain until 1989. First was Prague, where they had played in their last European tour in 1990. They had been wildly welcomed then, and that was the case again in 1995. Three nights later they played, for the first time, in Hungary, at the large Nepstadion in Budapest.

The tour then went to Germany, with appearances in stadiums in Schuttorf in western Germany, then performances in Leipzig in the former east and the united Berlin in the 1936 Olympic Stadium. There were shows in Hockenheim and Mannheim in southwest Germany before a concert in Wolfsburg in the north central part of the country. The concert on August 25 was in a central plaza in the city, which is the home of Volkswagen, one of the tour sponsors. After that, the tour played a concert in Luxembourg and two in Rotterdam, closing the tour on August 30 after more than a year.

The Voodoo Lounge Tour played to more than 6.5 million people and grossed more than $320 million, the highest-grossing tour ever.

The Stones were even more secure financially than before and could have slowed down, but the great success of the album and tour and the great fun that they had had actually made them eager to plan their next album and tour.

Following the tour, Don Was worked with Keith and Mick to mix the recordings from the three live sessions that had been made in Amsterdam, Paris, and London with the studio recordings made in Tokyo and Lisbon. The result was called *Stripped,* an "unplugged" album that had grown out of the *Unplugged* series on MTV that first featured Jethro Tull in 1987 then included many rock stars playing unamplified or acoustic concerts. *Stripped* was released in November 1995 and included 14 songs, five of which were not by Keith and Mick, though one of those was an old Nanker Phelge song, "The Spider and the Fly." The album was well reviewed and rose to number 9 in both the U.K. and U.S. charts. The Stones also released a single from the album, their version of Dylan's "Like a Rolling Stone," which got to number 12 in the United Kingdom and number 16 in the United States.

At the end of the year (1995), the Stones again went their own ways. Charlie released a solo jazz album, *Long Ago and Far Away,* in June 1996 and toured a bit in support of it. Ronnie recorded with Bo Diddley for an album released in 1996 and toured with him. Mick and Jerry Hall had their continued ups and downs. Mick acted in the film *Bent* during 1996, which was released in 1997. Keith went home to Weston, Connecticut, where Patti was very involved with the community and their two children were enrolled in a private Christian school. Keith stayed a while, then felt the pull to Jamaica, where he had recorded and lived in the 1970s. He recorded with a Rastafarian group he dubbed the Wingless Angels and also with Levon Helm (from the Band). Those albums were released in 1997. In May 1996, Keith joined Mick as a grandfather when his son Marlon's wife gave birth to a daughter, Ella Rose.

In summer 1996 Mick and Keith met and discussed a new album and agreed that they would also try a new format whereby each would have final say in the cutting of some tracks. Mick interpreted this as allowing him to bring in his own producer for each number, something Keith had not envisioned. Instead he had thought Don Was would again work with the two of them as coproducers. Thus there were a number of producers on the new album, titled *Bridges to Babylon.* Besides Keith and Mick (the Glimmer Twins) and Don Was, there were also Rob Fraboni, Danny Saber, Pierre de Beauport, and the "Dust Brothers" (Michael Simpson and John King). The album also featured a number of studio musicians playing bass and keyboards, possibly a reflection of the number of producers. There was a lot of disagreement between Keith and Mick, and at one point, Mick walked out of the studio, leaving Keith in charge.

Despite all the tension and the large number of people involved, the album was done in a surprisingly short amount of time over spring and summer 1997. The album was recorded and mixed at Ocean Way Studios in Los Angeles, with the release on September 29, 1997. The name of the album and the name of the upcoming tour grew out of Mick's interest in bridges and from discussing various title ideas with Tom Stoppard, the British playwright.

The album is uneven but continues much of the strength of the previous *Voodoo Lounge* album. *Bridges to Babylon* went to number 6 in the United Kingdom and number 3 in the United States and sold 4 million copies in the first year. Four singles were released from the album, and all went into the Top 100 charts with "Anybody Seen My Baby," the highest, at number 3. "Too Tight" and "Out of Control" are hard-driving songs in the best Stones tradition, while "Already Over Me" and "How Can I Stop" are songs that carry on lovely acoustical possibilities.

The Bridges to Babylon Tour was announced in August 1997 beneath the Brooklyn Bridge, with Manhattan as a backdrop. The tour motto was "Proves the world's best band is just that." Before the tour began, the band rehearsed in the Toronto area as they had for the Voodoo Lounge Tour, but this time in the Masonic Temple on Yonge Street. Again they had two open rehearsals in small clubs. First was in Toronto, in the Horseshoe Tavern, located in downtown Toronto and a music venue since 1947. The building itself was built in 1861, when it housed a blacksmith's shop. Close to 300 fans were able to squeeze in for the performance on September 4, 1997. The Stones played about a dozen songs in a 70-minute set, beginning around 11:00 P.M. The band played only two new songs from the *Bridges to Babylon* album, but they enjoyed the gig in the small club a great deal. Mick noted that a live audience was better than a week of private rehearsals, so the band decided the day before to do this with no publicity or real announcements.

The Stones returned to rehearsing before playing another club gig two weeks later on September 18, in Chicago at the Double Door. Again the decision was made the night before and received no publicity but a sign on the door at 9:00 A.M. saying "Rolling Stones tonight." Fans flocked to the club. Four hundred were admitted, leaving space for television and radio equipment. The band began playing at 10:00 P.M. and went through a set of 13 songs, with 3 from the new album.

The tour was scheduled to begin four nights later in Chicago's Soldier Field, and the Stones wanted to play there in a rehearsal before opening the tour. On September 19, despite heavy rain, the Stones were able to do most of their set, and they did the remainder on Sunday, September 21. On September 22, they went over a number of songs or sections of songs that weren't quite perfect, and on the day of the concert, September 23, the Stones rehearsed on a smaller, center stage before the gates opened. Whatever critics might think, the Stones worked hard to prepare their performances so that they could be near perfect.

Various acts opened for the Stones on the tour. These included Sheryl Crow, Foo Fighters, Smashing Pumpkins, Dave Matthews, Matchbox 20, Fiona Apple, Third Eye Blind, Blues Traveler, and the Wallflowers, depending on the city. The stage set was again designed by Mark Fisher and was based on the imagined desert city of the album cover. There was also a 1,600-square-foot eye-shaped JumboTron screen, which allowed for those even in the far reaches of the stadium to see the stage and action better than ever. The bridge that was installed by the eighth concert arched over the crowd to a small center stage at the back of the crowd.

The first concert was well received, especially the songs that were performed on the small center stage (the B stage), which provided an appearance of intimacy. The small bridge was not ready yet, so the band walked on a catwalk to the center stage, despite concerns about safety and security. One novelty to this tour was the ability of fans to vote (via the Internet) on a song (from a list of 20) to be played during the performance as song 10. The first night it was "Under My Thumb" and the second night it was "She's a Rainbow." From Chicago, the next performance was in Columbus at Ohio Stadium.

Three nights after that, the tour was in Winnipeg, Manitoba, then in Edmonton, Alberta, two nights after that. The band then played four concerts in six nights in football stadiums in Madison, Buffalo, Charlotte, and Philadelphia before doing two dates in Giants Stadium in East Rutherford, New Jersey, on October 16 and 17. Three nights later, they opened in Foxboro, Massachusetts, for two shows, then played in Landover, Maryland; Port Chester, New York; Nashville; Norman, Oklahoma; and Albuquerque, New Mexico. That ended the month of October, and the Stones opened November in Texas at the Texas Motor Speedway in Ft. Worth. There were six days off before opening in California, first in Dodgers Stadium in Los Angeles for two shows, then on to Oakland and Alameda Stadium for four more. The Stones closed out November with shows at the MGM Garden Arena in Las Vegas, the Metrodome in Minneapolis, and the Kingdome in Seattle.

Four days later, the tour was back in the East in another dome, the Silverdome in Pontiac, Michigan. Then the movement was south as the temperatures cooled. There were performances in the Orange Bowl in Miami, the Citrus Bowl in Orlando, and the Georgia Dome in Atlanta. The next show, on December 12, in the TWA Dome in St. Louis, was recorded, shown on pay-per-view, and released as a DVD. On December 13, Mick's second son, Gabriel, was born to Jerry Hall. After the St. Louis show, the tour broke for the remainder of the year.

After three weeks off, the tour continued in Quebec City before 15,000 at the Coliseum on January 5. This served as a kind of warm-up for the three performances in Madison Square Garden in New York on January 14, 16, and 17. Following the show, the Stones and their equipment flew to Hawaii for three shows in Honolulu on January 21, 23, and 24. One of the concerts was a private, beach resort affair for Pepsi employees for which the band received a reported $3 million. Then everything was packed up once again and flown back to Vancouver for a show on January 28 at BC Place Stadium. From there the tour went back to the United States, to Portland, for two shows in the Rose Garden Arena.

The final segments of the North American part of the tour were all in warmer climes. San Diego's Qualcomm Stadium was the venue on February 3, and then the tour went to Mexico for two shows in Mexico City. The final dates for North America were in Houston for two shows in the Summit Arena, then the Joint, outside Las Vegas, a smaller club venue that sat no more than 1,500, ended the tour leg on February 15. The 52 performances got great reviews, and the Stones looked forward to another month off before regrouping for the Japanese tour.

On March 12 the Stones opened in the Tokyo Dome and played four performances in six nights before traveling to Osaka, where they did two more on March 20 and 21. The Stones played to more than 200,000 spectators in their six shows in 10 days. Eight days later the tour was in South America, opening in Buenos Aires and playing five shows in eight days. After six off days they played two shows in Brazil, one in Rio de Janeiro and one in Sao Paulo. Bob Dylan opened for the Stones on these latter two shows and also joined them to sing "Like a Rolling Stone," which he had written. Nearly 350,000 attended the seven South American performances.

Four nights after playing in Brazil, the Stones were back in North America, giving five performances in 10 days in the Carrier Dome in Syracuse, the Molson Center in Montreal (two shows), the United Center in Chicago, and SkyDome in Toronto, closing on April 26.

June 1998 would start the European segment of the tour, nearly three years after they had last played on the Continent for the Voodoo Lounge Tour. This next part of the tour would go into September, and there would be 39 concerts in 19 countries before the last show on September 19 in Istanbul, Turkey. The summer shows were mostly at stadiums, but there were also some at large festival grounds. There was an unexpected setback when Keith had a bookshelf and dozens of books fall on him in his library while the tour was on break in May. He broke three ribs, and the opening show in Lyon was canceled. Instead the opener was in Nuremberg, Germany, on June 13. Then there were two shows at the Werchter Rock Festival in Belgium on June 20 and 21, followed by two shows in Germany (Hannover and Dusseldorf), which preceded a relatively long stay in Amsterdam. From June 29 to July 6, the Stones remained in Amsterdam and gave five performances at the 68,000-seat Amsterdam Arena, which had just opened in 1996.

Over the next week, there were concerts in Switzerland (Frauenfeld), Austria (Wiener Neustadt), and southern Germany (Munich's Olympic Stadium). Through much of the European tour, there were heavy rains, which made a mess of the fields and led to unanticipated consequences, most notably Mick's laryngitis, which forced the cancellation of some concerts. The tour continued in Spain in Malaga, Vigo, and Barcelona, but shows in Bilbao and Gijon as well as Marseilles were canceled. Only one rather than two Paris performances were played before the Stones headed to Gelsenkirchen in west central Germany and on to the Nordic countries.

Performances were given in Copenhagen, Gothenburg, Oslo, and Helsinki at the end of July and early August 1998. Then the Stones traveled to Eastern Europe for shows in countries that had never had gigantic rock concerts like this tour. First was Tallinn, Estonia, on August 8, and then the Stones fulfilled one of Keith's dreams by playing in Russia, in Moscow's 83,000-seat Luzhnicki Stadium. For nearly 30 years the Stones had tried to do a gig in Moscow but had always been refused because they were deemed too "decadent." The next stop was Chorzow, Poland, about 40 miles northwest of Krakow. The Stones then had six days before playing again in Zagreb, Croatia. The gap was filled by most of them returning to England for a giant party for Keith's daughter Angela.

Angela, his 26-year-old daughter by Anita Pallenberg, was married in Chichester on August 14 to Dominic Jennings, but Keith was unable to attend because of the concert that night in Poland. That date could not be changed, but a hiatus was inserted before the next concert in Zagreb. Keith flew back with Ronnie, though Mick and Charlie had to remain outside the country for tax reasons. Anita came with Marianne Faithfull. The wedding band included Keith, Ronnie, Darryl Jones, Bobby Keys, Bernard Fowler, and Lisa Fischer. Keith had arranged the bash for Redlands and had the local priest there redo the vows. Keith, Ronnie, Lisa, and Bernard rejoined the Stones tour in Zagreb, then the band went on to Prague, Berlin, and Leipzig before heading back to western Germany for concerts in Hamburg and Bremen, the latter on September 2.

Most of the remaining concerts in northern Europe were indoors, as the weather cooled in The Hague, Stockholm, Berlin, and Mannheim. On September 16, the Stones played the Olympic Stadium in Athens and closed the tour on September 19 in Istanbul's Ali Sami Yen Stadium.

The entire Bridges to Babylon Tour was just over one year and included travel to 25 countries for 109 performances, which were seen by over 4.6 million people. The gross for the tour was nearly $300 million, a simply astounding amount. If the Voodoo Lounge Tour had made the Stones financially set for life, the Bridges to Babylon Tour made them rich for two lifetimes! But it was not the money that drove them. Just as it was in 1963 when Keith, Brian, and Mick lived in the mess of Edith Grove, London, it was the music that made them continue to pursue a horrendously draining tour schedule, even in their middle to late 50s. The rush of audience excitement when Keith played the opening chords to "Satisfaction," as he did in each concert, still got the Stones going. Thus it was not surprising that the band decided to extend the tour into 1999.

Before making that decision, the band mixed a new album, drawn from the concerts on the 1997–1998 tour. This was their sixth official live album, and they took great care in selecting songs that had not been on prior live releases. This album, titled *No Security*, was released on November 2, 1998. The album peaked at number 67 in the United Kingdom and number 34 in the United States and sold over 300,000 copies. The new tour, to begin in January 1999, was initially meant to support this album, but the venues would all be arenas in North America. A continuation of the Bridges to Babylon Tour in large stadiums was contemplated for summer 1999. There was still life in the Rolling Stones.

NOTE

1. Kris Needs (2004), *Keith Richards: Before They Make Me Run,* London: Plexus, p. 302; Stephen Davis (2001), *Old Gods Almost Dead: The 40-Year Odyssey of the Rolling Stones,* New York: Broadway Books, p. 528. Crohn's disease is generally not fatal, but it is chronic and can take years off a person's life. Apparently Hopkins had such severe pain that an intestinal operation was tried to relieve some of the pain, and he died from the surgery.

CHAPTER NINE

No Security, 40 Licks, and *A Bigger Bang:* The Stones Won't Slow Down

Following the holidays of 1998, the band got back together in San Francisco in mid-January 1999 for 12 days of rehearsal for the upcoming No Security Tour, which was to begin in Oakland on January 25. The stage set was quite basic and was set up for a 360 degree view for the audience. There were no fireworks or light shows, just the music in a more intimate setting than the prior stadium tours. To be sure, this was still a show in large arenas of 15,000 to 20,000, but the show was the music, not all the other extras that had characterized the larger tours. Tickets were $40 to $75 face value, more than the bigger stadium ticket prices, though scalpers were getting as much as $250 or more for them. Surprisingly, some shows did not sell out. Besides the Stones, the only other performers were Darryl Jones on bass, Chuck Leavell on keyboards, Bobby Keys on sax, and Blondie Chapin as backup vocalist.

The playlist was 22 to 25 songs per show, and many of the songs selected had not lent themselves to being played in a big stadium performance like those of *Bridges to Babylon* or *Voodoo Lounge*. Following Oakland, the tour did two more shows in California, in Sacramento and San Jose, before moving to Denver and Salt Lake City for gigs there. Then it was back to California for another show in Sacramento and two in Anaheim.

Four nights later, on February 15, the Stones began a tour of the upper Midwest with stops in Minneapolis, Fargo, Milwaukee, Detroit, and Toronto. Most of the shows were in basketball or hockey arenas. The tour swung south with two shows in Tampa and Sunrise (near Ft. Lauderdale), Florida, in the beginning of March. Then it was on to Washington, D.C., for two shows at the MCI Center, followed by shows in Pittsburgh and Philadelphia at the First Union (now Wachovia) Center.

After a trip to Charlotte, the tour went back north for two shows in Boston at the Fleet Center (now TD Banknorth Garden). A stop in Chicago's United Center was followed by two shows in Hartford's Civic Arena, then two shows in Ohio to begin April. The first was in the Gund (now Quicken Loans) Arena in Cleveland, and the second was in Columbus at the Value City Arena. The Midwestern swing continued with shows in Kansas City, Memphis, and Oklahoma City before a return to Chicago for another show on April 12.

The tour ended with shows back West, in Las Vegas at the MGM Grand Arena and two in San Jose Arena, closing on April 20, 1999. There were a total of 34 shows with just under 575,000 paid attendees. Crowd sizes ranged from 12,500 to just over 20,000.

A month later, the tour continued in Europe as the extension of the Bridges to Babylon Tour of the year before. In the prior year, four shows in England had been canceled at the behest of the Stones' financial adviser, Prince Rupert Lowenstein. Because of revised British tax law, the Stones (and their entire traveling entourage) would have been subject to more than £12 million (almost $20 million) of tax liability had they played the scheduled dates in England in summer 1998. Thus they were deferred until the extended tour for June 1999.

The shortened leg of the Bridges to Babylon Tour only ran for three weeks. Opening date was May 29 in Stuttgart, followed by a festival in Imst, Austria, and a show in Groningen, Netherlands, on June 2.

At this point the band headed to England to do the shows that had been canceled in 1998. They did performances in Edinburgh and Sheffield, followed by three in London. The first was in Shepherd's Bush Empire, a music hall built in 1903. This was the club date of the tour, with just 1,200 tickets sold at £10 per ticket. Two shows in Wembley Stadium were performed on June 11 and 12. The final three shows of the tour were in Santiago de Compostela in the Galician region of Spain, Landgraaf in southern Netherlands, and Cologne,

Germany, on June 20. Taking the entire Bridges to Babylon/No Security tours as a whole, the band had played over 150 venues in just under two years. The total gross was over $300 million. During that time there had been many changes, most notably to Mick. He and Jerry had a new child, Gabriel, born in December 1997 when the tour was in the United States. Then, in August 1999, just after the end of the tour, the marriage of Mick and Jerry was annulled (though it had not been recognized in the United States and United Kingdom). Jerry had filed for divorce, and Mick's lawyers countered by saying that the marriage was invalid. The marriage had always been difficult since Mick simply did not believe in monogamy.[1] The final blow for Jerry was when Luciana Gimenez, a 28-year-old Brazilian model, gave birth to a son, Lucas, on May 18, 1999, with Mick as the father. He and Luciana ended their relationship later that year.

The Stones would not tour for another three years, and their next album would be released concurrent with that tour in 2002. Despite this, the Stones had lots of their own projects to pursue, as they had during the last big hiatus in the early 1990s. Charlie toured with his jazz band. Mick's mother died in May 2000, but Mick returned to the studio and began recording in early 2000, then intermittently from January to July 2001. He released his fourth solo album, *Goddess in the Doorway*, which he also coproduced, in November 2001. The album got some excellent reviews, though sales were not as impressive but still respectable. It went to number 39 in the United Kingdom, with eight weeks in the Top 200; to number 44 in the United States, with four weeks in the Top 75; and to number 6 on the Eurocharts, with nine weeks in the Top 100. Worldwide sales topped 1 million as of March 2002.

Ronnie was having troubles with alcohol, cocaine, and money management. He invested a great deal in a club in London that was a spectacular failure, draining Wood's bank account, such that he had to borrow from the Stones and bring in a new and more disciplined manager, his son Jamie. Ronnie's son brought the Wood spending under control, but Woody was still in need of rehab, which he finally underwent in Cottonwood, Arizona, after a stay at a rehab center in England. The Arizona rehab was done just before the next Stones tour, which would also allow Ronnie to have shows of his art at various galleries along the tour.[2]

Keith had a difficult time with personal losses during this period between Stones tours. His father died as well as a number of close friends, most notably George Harrison, who died in Los Angeles of lung cancer in November 2001. As Ronnie's best mate, Keith was both sympathetic and empathetic regarding Woody's addictions and need for rehab. He would support Ron throughout the upcoming tour, a tour that the Stones were not sure initially that Ronnie would be able to undertake.

In May 2002 the band got together in Paris to record new material for another compilation album, *40 Licks,* which would celebrate 40 years of the band. Mick, Keith, and Charlie had had discussions earlier about such an album and determined what earlier songs should be included. Ronnie was involved with providing input into songs of which he had been a part. Some songs were remixed, others rerecorded with new mixing, and four new songs were made. Of those new songs, one, "Don't Stop," was also released as a single. It ultimately reached number 21 and number 36 in the United States and United Kingdom, respectively. The other new cuts, "Keys to Your Love," "Stealing My Heart," and "Losing My Touch," would be well received on tour and made interest in the album greater. The album was released on September 30–October 1 and rose to number 2 in both the U.K. and U.S. charts, ultimately selling 8 million copies.

The new 40 Licks Tour was announced in May 2002 in New York City's Van Cortland Park. The Stones arrived at the press conference in a yellow blimp with their trademark lips-and-tongue logo on the side. The tour would begin in the fall, just as the new album was released. The plans for the tour would be altered, however, because of the worldwide SARS epidemic, which emerged as a near-pandemic from November 2002 to July 2003. Spreading outward from China, SARS affected 37 countries before being declared fully contained in May 2006 by the World Health Organization.

The band again assembled for tour rehearsals in the Toronto area. This would be an unusual tour in that there would be few new songs to promote, but that allowed for a vast playlist, which reached 80 songs by the time the tour ended. As usual, the Stones played about 25 songs per concert, but the venues were mixed among stadiums, arenas, and clubs, and that affected the choice of songs to be played.

The warm-up concert was played in Toronto at the Palais Royale Ballroom. Unlike prior years, news of this date leaked out much earlier than the day of the concert, and fans queued up for days for tickets to the August 16 performance. The venue had been built in the early 1900s and hosted the big bands of the 1930s like Count Basie's. Capacity was around 2,000, and the club was packed for the Stones' appearance, with fans paying just $10 each. For the first time, Ronnie

The Rolling Stones in front of their blimp in Van Cortland Park, New York City, in May 2002, where they announced the opening of the 40 Licks Tour to begin in September: from left, Charlie Watts, Mick Jagger, Ronnie Wood, and Keith Richards. (AP-02050702558)

was playing a tour while sober, and it made him and the rest of the Stones a bit nervous, not knowing what to expect. But Ronnie found new focus in sobriety, and the result was great both for his playing and for his confidence.

The official opening to the tour was in Boston with shows on September 3, 5, and 8. In a pattern that would be repeated in a number of cities, the Stones played in a stadium (Gillette in Foxboro), an arena (the Fleet Center), and a club/theater (the Orpheum, a music hall opened in 1852 and located just off Boston Common). In Chicago the pattern was repeated with shows at the United Center, Comiskey Park, and the Aragon Ballroom (an enormous ballroom on the north side of Chicago with a capacity of more than 10,000 for shows).

The next stop was Philadelphia, where the band played in Veterans Stadium, the First Union Center Arena, and the Tower Theatre in Upper Darby, six miles from center city in Delaware County. Then the Stones went to New York for a week, where the three venues were Madison Square Garden, Giants Stadium in New Jersey, and the Roseland Ballroom. This latter venue is on West 52nd, close to the Stones' hotel and not far from where Keith, Mick, and Ron had homes. It can accommodate up to 3,000 standing customers. This concert mixed a lot of songs not usually played in stadiums and arenas, and the "real" Stones fans were delighted. After New York the pattern was a bit different.

On October 4 the band played in Landover, Maryland, at 90,000-seat FedEx Field, and the next night, they played in the Hartford Civic Center before taking a week off. They regrouped on October 12 to begin a series of performances at upper midwestern venues: Ford Field in Detroit, Gund Arena in Cleveland, Air Canada Centre in Toronto, Rogers Centre (formerly SkyDome) in Toronto, and Nationwide Arena in Columbus.

Then the tour dropped into the South with shows in Sunrise and Miami, Florida, and Atlanta before another break of five days to get set up in California for a show in the Staples Center in Los Angeles. This was the first of eight West Coast shows in a two-week period. After Los Angeles, Anaheim's Edison International Field followed on November 2, then, two days later, the Wiltern Theatre in the Koreatown section of Los Angeles. The Wiltern was built in 1931, and the ballroom holds about 2,000. The band moved up to the Tacoma Dome then back to the Bay Area to do two shows in Pacific Bell Park in San Francisco and one in the Oakland Arena before performing at the San Diego Sports Arena.

The Stones played San Diego on November 14 then didn't do another public show until November 23 in the SBC Center in San Antonio. They did do a show in between, however, and that was at the Joint, a 4,000-seat showroom inside the Hard Rock Casino in Paradise, Nevada, just outside Las Vegas. The performance, which was 90 minutes long, was for a private party celebrating the 60th birthday of a wealthy entrepreneur named David Bonderman. This was not a common occurrence, but for $7 million, the Stones agreed to the private appearance. The Stones were preceded by John Mellencamp, who played for an hour.

A week later, on November 23, the Stones played in San Antonio then went to Nashville, to the 20,000-seat Gaylord Entertainment Center, after which they returned to Las Vegas, where they played the Joint on November 29 and the MGM Grand Garden Arena on November 30.

During the summer of 2002, just before the tour began, it was announced that Mick would be receiving a knighthood from the queen of England after being recommended by Prime Minister Tony Blair. This caused some rancor within the Stones. Keith found it distasteful and antithetical to the image of the Rolling Stones. He was quite adamant in his feeling that Mick should refuse the offer of knighthood, which Keith certainly would have done. Mick was happy to accept since he had become so close to many of the royals through Princess Margaret, and he saw himself as a businessman now, as much as a musician. Charlie thought Keith should have been offered a knighthood also, though he knew that Keith would have refused immediately. The whole issue revived the love-hate relationship between Keith and Mick.

The tour broke for the holidays and reconvened in Montreal's Bell Center on January 8, 2003. The rest of the 40 Licks Tour, with one exception, would be at arenas of 15,000 to 20,000 seating capacity. Performances were at the Mellon Center in Pittsburgh, the Fleet Center in Boston, two shows in Madison Square Garden, and two in Chicago's United Center, before the performance in Houston's Reliant Stadium before 70,000 on January 25. Shows in Oklahoma City and Phoenix ended January, and concerts in Denver, San Jose, Los Angeles, and Las Vegas ended this leg of the tour on February 8, 2003. The tour grossed over $120 million in just over four months and 50 shows. Ronnie had a gallery show of his paintings in New York that coincided with the Madison Square Garden concerts. He also had shows in galleries in San Francisco and Los Angeles in the fall, when the band had played in California.

There was a brief time off, but most of it was spent traveling then acclimating to Australia for the next leg of the tour, beginning on February 18 in Sydney. The opener was at the Enmore Theatre, in the Newtown section of Sydney. The club had a capacity of 2,000, and the tickets were sold out in December. The Stones did a club show with a lot of less-played numbers. Then they did two more shows at the Superdome in Sydney before heading to Melbourne for three shows at the Rod Laver Arena, with a capacity of just under 15,000. The last Australian shows were in Brisbane on March 4 and 5 at the Brisbane Entertainment Centre in the suburb of Boondall.

Five days later the band opened their Japan tour with a performance in the Nippon Budokan, built for the martial arts competition of the 1964 Olympics and seating about 14,000. Then they played at the Yokohama Arena, about 25 miles from Tokyo, before doing two shows in the Tokyo Dome on March 15 and 16, in front of more than 50,000 at each show. The Stones ended the Japan tour with two shows in Osaka at the Osaka Dome then flew to Singapore to do two shows in the Indoor Stadium there, with about 12,000 at each show.

The trip to Singapore was a first for the band, but even more excit-ing was the prospect of their first appearance in China. Unfortunately, all four shows in China (two in Hong Kong, one in Shanghai, and one in Beijing) had to be canceled because of the SARS epidemic. This was also true of the planned concert in Thailand. Instead the Stones played two concerts in India in April, at the Palace Grounds in Bangalore before 30,000 (April 4) and at Brabourne Stadium in Mumbai before 20,000 (April 10).

Then the Stones had nearly two months off before beginning the European part of the tour in June. Munich's Olympiahalle (used for gymnastics and team handball in the 1972 Olympics and seating about 14,000) was the venue for the first European concert of the 40 Licks Tour. The band played in the Olympic Stadium and, finally, com-pleted the trilogy in Munich with a performance at Circus Krone, an old circus building in downtown Munich that accommodated 2,400 spectators in blistering heat (which was matched by a blisteringly hot performance).

The Stones did shows in Milan and Oberhausen (Germany), followed by stadium shows in Berlin and Vienna. Then they played a festival in Leipzig and at an auto racetrack in Hockenheim in southwestern Germany on June 22. Three concerts in three Spanish stadiums (Bilbao, Madrid, and Barcelona) followed, after which they played a stadium in Marseilles before doing a trio of shows in Paris. The first was in Palais Omnisport de Bercy, an arena, followed by a concert in the national stadium of France and a third in the Paris Olympia, a music hall in the Ninth District.

The tour went north to the Nordic countries, where there were concerts in Copenhagen and Helsinki before the band did another trio of performances, this time in the Stockholm area. First there was one in the Olympic Stadium, then one at the Globe Arena. The club venue was the Circus Arena, which held just over 1,500 people. The Stones then did shows in Hamburg and Prague before taking a break from the European tour. The day before the Prague performance was Mick's 60th birthday, July 26, 2003.

On July 30 the band was back in Toronto to do a benefit concert for both SARS and the city of Toronto, which had had an outbreak of SARS (and was under a health warning from the World Health Organization) and had lost millions in income from canceled trips to the city. The entire city was depressed over the way it was now being viewed internationally, and the Stones wanted to alter that perception. Toronto had been the rehearsal locale and the scene of great concerts for the Stones as well as where Keith had to face his addiction problems, so the band was eager to be the driving force in the creation of an enormous concert to be held in Downsview Park in north Toronto, where 800,000 had welcomed Pope Paul II in 2002.

Titled Molson Rocks for Toronto, there were three parts to the concert, which drew between 450,000 and 500,000 to the park. (One official total had the number at just over 489,000, a record for a paying event.[3]) The afternoon session had nine acts, including the Isley Brothers, and was hosted by Dan Ackroyd. Each act had 15 to 20 minutes, after which there was a break before the second part began in the late afternoon and included Justin Timberlake, the Guess Who, AC/DC, and Rush. Then the Stones closed the concert with a 90-minute performance. The Stones also spent some time in the city before returning to Europe, where they resumed the 40 Licks Tour on August 8 in Hannover, Germany. From there they went to the Netherlands, where they did five shows, the first three of which were in Rotterdam. Two were in a stadium, but the third was in an arena seating 10,000. Then they went to Utrecht and played at a small music hall (1,800 capacity), Vrendenburg, in central Utrecht, where the reception and performance were exceptional. Three nights later (August 19), they did their last Dutch show at the Amsterdam Arena and spent a few more days in Amsterdam before heading to the United Kingdom for nine performances in a month.

The first shows in London would follow the three-venue pattern of other large cites that had been established early in the tour, but this set of shows would be different. The tour and the album were a commemoration of 40 years of the Stones, but it was in England, specifically London, where the Stones had started. Being back on that turf, 40 years later, was a very powerful and emotional event for the band. The first show was in Twickenham Stadium in London on August 24, and three nights later the band played at the Astoria (now closed) on Charing Cross Road in London before about 2,000, and tickets were hard to find since so many celebrities wanted to see and be seen there. Two nights later, the Stones played the 12,500-seat Wembley Arena.

The Stones left London and did two shows in Glasgow at the Scottish Exhibition and Conference Center, seating 3,000, then did a show in Manchester at the large arena there. There was a fast jaunt to Belgium for a performance in Werchter Park, before flying to Ireland to do two shows in Dublin at the Point Theatre, a concert hall seating about 8,500.

On September 13 and 15, the Stones gave two performances at Wembley Arena, where they had appeared two weeks earlier. The Stones then did another stadium show at Twickenham before heading back to Amsterdam for another show in the Amsterdam Arena on September 22. The last week of the tour consisted of two shows in Spain (Benidorm and Zaragoza) and one in Coimbra, Portugal, before the European tour ended in Letzigrund Stadium in Zurich, Switzerland, on October 2, 2003.

The Stones went back to China the next month to do two concerts, making up, in a way, for those shows that were canceled by the SARS outbreak. The two performances were both in Hong Kong at the Tamar site on the harbor, on November 7 and 9.

The 40 Licks Tour had covered almost 16 months (including breaks). The Stones had visited 23 countries and done 116 shows, almost all totally sold out. There were approximately 3.4 million concert attendees, and the tour grossed about $300 million. The band was the number one rock attraction in the world and one of the few to tour the world to prove it. The pace had been exhausting for anyone, even more remarkable when one considers that Charlie had his 62nd birthday on the tour, Mick his 60th, and that Keith would be 60 the next December. Ronnie, the youngster, celebrated his 56th birthday on the tour.

On December 12, Mick Jagger's official entry into knighthood was completed at Buckingham Palace. Though announced in 2002, it took 18 months for Mick to find the time to be knighted. Mick's 90-year-old father, Joe, and two of his daughters, Karis and Elizabeth, attended the ceremony. The queen was recovering from knee surgery, so Prince Charles did the actual knighting.

Nine months later, in September 2004, the Stones began recording a new album in France, mostly at Mick's house, with Don Was again producing with Mick and Keith. Other recordings and mixes were done in the Caribbean at Mick's home in Mustique. Charlie was not as involved with the mixes as in some previous albums as he was recovering from radiation treatments for throat cancer, diagnosed in June 2004. Subsequently, the cancer went into remission, and there have been no reported recurrences as of 2009.

In November 2004, the Stones' seventh live album, *Live Licks,* was released and contained songs drawn from the 40 Licks Tour of 2002–2003. This was a double album with 24 songs on the discs, and it was well received for a live album, rising to number 38 in the United Kingdom and number 50 in the United States but going gold in sales.

Mick Jagger with his father, Joe, and daughters Karis (with Marsha Hunt) and Elizabeth (with Jerry Hall) after the ceremony in Buckingham Palace where he was knighted by Prince Charles on December 12, 2003. (AP-03121203284)

Meanwhile Ronnie was back to selling his artwork but was also drinking again. Charlie was relaxing at home, where his wife liked to listen to Stones music, but he did not. Keith continued to be a homebody in Connecticut but would escape to the Caribbean at times. Sir Mick did some music for film and pursued various music and acting gigs. His song "Old Habits Die Hard," for the remake of the film *Alfie,* won a Golden Globe for best original song (music was by David Stewart, who shared the award). Mick had also taken on a new lady friend, L'Wren Scott (born Luann Bambrough in Utah in 1967), who was a fashion and costume designer and former model. She designed Mick's wardrobe for the Bigger Bang Tour.

Final mixes of the new album, *A Bigger Bang,* were completed in June 2005. At that time the Stones also announced, at New York's Julliard School of Music, a new tour, which would promote the album. They played a few songs to add to the festivities. As for the question of whether this would be the Stones' final tour, Mick did not think that to be the case. The Bigger Bang Tour would commence in August 2005, so the Stones went, once again, to the Toronto area to begin their rehearsals. They again rehearsed at a private school and did large stage rehearsals at an empty hangar at the Pearson International Airport outside Toronto.

As had become customary, the Stones did a club date 10 days before the actual tour began. This time they chose the Phoenix Concert Theatre on Sherburne Street, not far from the University of Toronto. The club has a capacity of about 1,000, and it was filled on August 10, 2005, for the Stones' performance. Unlike the 40 Licks Tour, which had only four new songs, this show would have a number of new songs from the *Bigger Bang* album, so rehearsals were a bit more taxing. The resulting show at the Phoenix, which ran nearly two hours, was a great success and sent the Stones off, eager to finish a week of rehearsals and get on the road.

Opening concerts were at Boston's Fenway Park on August 21 and 23, followed by a concert in a stadium in Hartford three days later and another stadium show in Ottawa a couple days after that, followed by a show at Comerica Park in Detroit. The tour was rolling, and it would end up being longer than planned, not ending for two years. The 40 Licks Tour had been different from previous tours in the playlists that were used, depending on venue size and what the Stones had played previously in that city. That pattern continued in the Bigger Bang Tour as the Stones varied their playlist by five or six songs each night and used archival records that Chuck Leavell had kept of what had been played in towns previously to offer those places a completely different show from prior visits.

The next concert, on September 3, was in Moncton, New Brunswick, at the Magnetic Hill concert site, originally built for the visit of Pope Paul II in 1984. The Stones drew the biggest crowd ever in Atlantic Canada with an estimated 85,000 at the concert, which ended at about 10:30 P.M. and opened with fireworks. The band then played at two indoor arenas in St. Paul, Minnesota, and Milwaukee, before giving a concert in Chicago's Soldier Field on September 10. Then they did two shows in the New York City area, one in Madison Square Garden and the other in Giants Stadium, before going upstate to Albany to perform at the Pepsi Arena there.

The tour traveled to Columbus to the Nationwide Arena, then to Toronto to the Rogers Centre, before doing four shows in stadiums in Pittsburgh, Hershey, Charlottesville, and Durham and one in the MCI Center in Washington, D.C. The cooler weather of October led to arena dates dominating the rest of the month. Tour stops were the Wachovia Center in Philadelphia for two shows and performances in Atlanta, Miami, Tampa, Charlotte, Calgary, Seattle, and Portland, though there was a week off in the midst of that run for recovery time.

The stops in California, beginning November 4, were all in outdoor stadiums, beginning in Anaheim, followed by two shows in the Hollywood Bowl (really more of an outdoor band shell with seating for over 17,000), Petco Park in San Diego, and two shows in SBC Park in San Francisco. The band played at the MGM Grand Arena in Las Vegas before returning to California for a performance at an arena in Fresno. November ended with shows in arenas in Salt Lake City; Denver; Glendale, Arizona; and Dallas. On December 1 the Stones played in Houston, then finished for 2005 in Memphis's FedEx Forum. The Stones had done 43 shows in just over 100 days, so they were happy to have a rest for a month, most of which would be spent at home or in the Caribbean.

The band regrouped early in January and rehearsed a bit in Canada before doing one show in Montreal. The rest of the tour in North America would all be in arenas and included two shows in Boston, two in Madison Square Garden, two in Chicago, and single shows in St. Louis, Omaha, Baltimore, Detroit, and Atlanta, which finished the North American leg of the tour on February 8. The show in Detroit was shorter than usual because it was done at the halftime of Super Bowl XL. The Stones sang three songs, two of which, "Start Me Up" and "Rough Justice," were censored because of sexual suggestiveness. "Satisfaction" was the third song in the 12-minute set.

From Atlanta, the Stones flew directly to Puerto Rico, where they gave their first concert ever on the island at the Coliseo de Puerto Rico in San Juan. Then the band flew to Brazil for some relaxation before continuing the tour at Copacabana Beach in Rio de Janeiro in a most unusual concert. The giant tour stage was assembled directly on the beach, and a walkway over the highway parallel to the beach was built to allow the band to walk right to the backstage area from their hotel. The stage was begun on February 15; the Stones arrived late on February 16, and the show was on February 18, before what was estimated to be 1 million fans. The concert was sponsored by two large telecommunications companies. The concert was broadcast on television and radio in Brazil and worldwide via the Internet. The Stones were paid $750,000 for the free concert, with the notion that a DVD would be produced from the concert.[4] After wowing Brazil, the Stones went to Argentina for two stadium shows in Buenos Aires then flew back north to give two concerts in Mexico City and Monterey, the latter on March 1, 2006.

Then it was back to the United States for 10 days as the Stones gave five concerts at the MGM Grand in Las Vegas, the Forum in Los Angeles, the ALLTEL Arena in north Little Rock, the Bank Atlantic Center in Sunrise, Florida, and Radio City Music Hall in New York City on March 14. This last show was the only benefit on the tour and was for the Robin Hood Foundation, a New York City antipoverty organization. Only 5,000 fans were able to get in the hall to hear a number of groups, and then the Stones did 19 numbers, a bit fewer than the usual show. Still, the intimacy made the show memorable. A week later the band began the Asia/Pacific leg of the tour.

Japan was the start of the Pacific tour, with five shows in two weeks. Two were in Tokyo, one in Sapporo on Hokkaido in northern Japan, one in the Saitama Super Arena, just north of Tokyo, and one in Nagoya, about 150 miles west of Tokyo. This performance was on April 5, and the only performance in China was on April 8 in Shanghai. This was historic in that the Stones had never played in China since their scheduled concerts in 2003 had been canceled because of SARS. They had managed to get to Hong Kong, however. Only 8,000 tickets were available for the Shanghai show, and some were reportedly going for $600 prior to the concert. China's Ministry of Culture forbade the playing of five songs (because of sexual suggestiveness), and the Stones complied. These were "Brown Sugar," "Let's Spend the Night Together," "Beast of Burden," "Rough Justice," and "Honky Tonk Women." In their first Chinese concert, most tickets were purchased by expatriates living in China since most Chinese could not afford to attend.

Three nights later the Rolling Stones played in Sydney, Australia, before doing a show in Melbourne two nights later. Then they flew to New Zealand for two more shows in Auckland and Wellington. The date was April 18, and it marked the end of the tour for three months after about eight months of touring. Mick remained in New Zealand to film a cameo for an American television show, *The Knights of Prosperity*. (The show was to be called *Let's Rob Mick Jagger*, but that was shelved, though Mick was a guest star.) Ronnie and his wife, Jo, as well as Keith and Patti went to Fiji. They had a great time kayaking, lying on the beach, and relaxing, but a freak accident nearly ended the tour and also nearly cost Keith Richards his life. While climbing a coconut tree to obtain coconuts, Keith fell and landed on his head. At first, he just had a headache but then became quite sick and was flown to a hospital in New Zealand with what was diagnosed as a blood clot beneath his skull. Surgery was performed to relieve the swelling.

To allow Keith time to recover, some shows in Europe were canceled (though most were subsequently rescheduled at the end of the tour).

With Keith recovered, the European part of the tour began on July 11 in Milan, where Keith sang "As Tears Go By" in Italian, and the band brought two of the members of the World Cup–winning Italian soccer team on stage to wild applause. This gig was followed by shows in Vienna, Munich, Hannover, Berlin, and Cologne, then shows in Paris and Amsterdam, before a return to Germany at Stuttgart on August 3. These were followed by performances in Zurich, Nice, and Oporto (Portugal) before the two shows scheduled for Spain had to be canceled because of Mick's laryngitis.

After eight days with no shows, Mick seemed fine, and the tour did five shows in the United Kingdom, two in London, one in Glasgow, one in Sheffield, and one in Cardiff, ending August 29, 2006. The band then did two final shows in Bergen, Norway, and in a small stadium in Horsens, Denmark (about 30 miles south of Arhus in western Denmark) on September 1 and 3, respectively.

The band then took three weeks off, which they clearly needed, before opening the return leg of the tour in North America at the end of September 2006. The first half of the tour was all performed at large outdoor venues, some of which had never previously held the Stones. The first show was in Gillette Stadium in Foxboro, Massachusetts, but the second was on the Halifax Common in central Halifax, Nova Scotia. The excitement of the Stones coming to Nova Scotia was played across the local newspapers from the time that the date was announced in July. Fifty thousand fans were there for the performance, which was preceded by a number of bands five hours before the Rolling Stones came on stage. Unfortunately, the entire concert was held in heavy rain, but the day was still memorable. The Stones had had all of their equipment waterproofed many years before for both cost and safety reasons, so the rain did not damage the equipment.

The next shows were in Giant Stadium near New York, Louisville, Wichita, Missoula, Regina, Chicago, Seattle, and El Paso. On October 22, the band played in Zilker Park in Austin, Texas, before 42,000 fans. Ian McLagan (formerly of Faces, with Ron Wood) and his Bump Band opened, followed by Los Lonely Boys, and then by the Rolling Stones. It was a thrill for the crowd and for the Stones, playing their first time in Austin, a noted music mecca.

The Stones then went to New York, where they rehearsed at the historic Beacon Theatre for two concerts there on October 29 and

November 1. The concerts were fundraisers for former president Bill Clinton's foundation, and both he and Hillary Clinton were in attendance. The concerts were recorded by Martin Scorsese as part of his documentary film on the concerts, titled *Shine a Light*. Recordings were also made for a live album, which the Stones released in 2008, also titled *Shine a Light*. An unfortunate incident at the first concert occurred when Ahmet Ertegun, the former Atlantic Records CEO who had signed the Stones to that company and remained friends with them, slipped and fell backstage and hurt his head. It was initially seen as minor, but he later slipped into a coma and died on December 1, a month later. Scorsese's film was dedicated to Ertegun.

A few days later, the tour continued with stadium shows in Oakland and Phoenix, then a show at the MGM Grand Arena in Las Vegas and one in the Idaho Center in Boise. There was a trip east for one show in Atlantic City before the Stones ended the North American segment with shows in Los Angeles and Vancouver on November 25, 2006.

The last part of the Bigger Bang Tour would be in Europe and would run 82 days and encompass 30 shows in 28 venues, which included 21 countries, some of which the Stones had not performed in previously. Some of the concerts were to be makeups for those lost to either Keith's injury or Mick's laryngitis the year before. All would be outdoors, except for the last three, and some of the new venues would be quite exciting.

The start of the tour was to be festival sites with performances at Werchter Park in Belgium, Goffert Park in the Netherlands, and the Isle of Wight Festival. The band rehearsed in Vilvoorde, outside Brussels, for a few weeks, then rehearsed at the Werchter site before opening on June 5 before 35,000.

From the festival settings, the Stones moved to stadium venues in Frankfort, Paris, Lyon, Barcelona, San Sebastian (on the Spanish coast just north of Pamplona), Lisbon, and Madrid. The last show in Iberia was in El Ejido, on the Mediterranean, about 100 miles east of Gibraltar. This was followed six days later with a stadium show in Rome. Then the tour began to visit Eastern Europe, places they had not played before. These included stadiums in Belgrade, Bucharest, Budapest, and Brno (Czech Republic) as well as a concert near the beach in Budva, Montenegro. Between these concerts, there was also a private show back in Barcelona for just 700 privileged guests of Deutsche Bank.

After that, there were two more shows in Eastern Europe, in Warsaw and St. Petersburg, where Keith had wanted to play for many years. This desire was finally a reality, as the band performed in the Palace Square before 40,000. The Stones then spent a week in the Nordic countries performing four concerts in Helsinki, Gothenburg, Copenhagen, and Oslo, before doing three shows in central Europe in Lausanne, Dusseldorf, and Hamburg. The Stones flew to Ireland and played before 70,000 outside Slane Castle, near Dublin, where they had also performed in 1982. The tour ended in London with three shows at the O2 Millennium Dome, an indoor arena seating 23,000, on August 21, 23, and 26.

In two years the Bigger Bang Tour had performed 146 shows in 32 countries, plus Puerto Rico and the Isle of Wight. The financial gross was a staggering $558 million, making it the all-time leader in tour sales ever. Second highest was U2's Vertigo Tour, at over $300 million, with the Stones' Voodoo Lounge and Bridges to Babylon tours being the third and fourth highest grosses ever. The Rolling Stones had earned both an enormous amount of money and the time to rest a bit on their laurels.

NOTES

1. Christopher Andersen (1993), *Jagger, Unauthorized*, New York: Delacorte Press, discusses this many times. Marianne Faithfull, with David Dalton (1994), *Faithfull: An Autobiography*, New York: Cooper Square Press, also notes this in her relationship with Jagger.
2. Ronnie Wood (2007), *Ronnie: The Autobiography*, New York: St. Martin's Griffin, chap. 31, pp. 305–16, discusses this in detail.
3. Wood, *Ronnie*, p. 315, citing local newspapers of the time. A number of Web sites support this contention but have no further substantiation. No official count seems to exist.
4. Robert Greenfield (2006), *Exile on Main Street: A Season in Hell with the Rolling Stones*, Cambridge, MA: Da Capo Press.

Afterword: The Stones Still Looking Forward

From August 2005 to August 2007 the Rolling Stones toured for 12 of the 25 months, circumnavigating the globe twice. Anyone who has traveled knows how debilitating it can be, yet these men, all in their late 50s and early 60s, not only traveled but put on exhausting rock concerts over 200 times during that period. In 2010 the Rolling Stones—Ronnie Wood, Keith Richards, Mick Jagger, and Charlie Watts—ranged in age from 62 to 69, a time when most people are retired or contemplating it. Yet there is no indication of an end to the band. How long and why would they continue?

One thing should be clear at this point, and that is that it isn't about the money, and it never has been. When the band began over 40 years ago and had no money, they continued to play because they loved to make music. The money was ancillary, and for many years, they didn't receive much of it. Today they have more money than any of them could spend, but it is still about the music that they love to create.

Marshall Chess, the former Stones confidant, claims that what gets the Stones revved up is still the "buzz that they get when they go on stage. It's like a drug. And the only way that they can get it is to go on tour.... It's the power. That's why these guys still do it."[1]

The band members genuinely love each other, and the Stones are a real family. They fight at times, they go their separate ways, they have their own interests, but they support each other in so many ways. Being in the band may be "just a job," but being a Rolling Stone is much more than that to each of them. Keith was so perplexed and angry over Bill Wyman quitting the band that he wanted to force him to play because Bill was a Rolling Stone, then, now, and forever. Nevertheless, the rest of the band let Bill quit, though he is still part of the family.

Many enterprises have spun off from the Stones' base as the band members did their own individual music, pursued other art forms like film or painting, and got involved in various other philanthropic causes. They have helped nurture new musical artists by having them open for tours or play back up on some of their recordings.

From scruffy, disparaged young musicians in the 1960s, they have become revered musical artists and are recognized worldwide as the greatest rock and roll band in history. The band has stayed together almost 50 years and recorded and released more than 60 albums, including 26 original studio albums. From covering great blues songs of American artists, they have produced songs that many have covered in homage to them. There is certainly nothing left to prove.

Nevertheless, every time that the Rolling Stones take the stage, they do have something to prove to themselves, that is, that they can still play the greatest music around. In Mozart's time, he was a rebel with his musical compositions and arrangements, but he died at 35, too early to be universally revered, as he would have been had he continued to produce music into his 60s. The Rolling Stones have been fortunate enough to live to be revered, and that in and of itself is amazing. Many friends and colleagues have passed away over the past 48 years, yet the Stones have endured, despite addictions, abuses, fires, falls, death threats, and diseases. They would agree that they have been very lucky as well as very talented.

But all this really begs the question, what now? The last appearance that the Rolling Stones made was in the 2008 Martin Scorsese film of the concert at the Beacon Theatre, which was part of the Bigger Bang Tour. Since that time they have not played together, but they have pursued different things. They did appear in both London and Berlin in early 2008 to promote the release of the film, though they did not play any music.

Ronnie Wood continues to paint and exhibit his artwork in galleries in the United States and Europe. He seems to have relapsed, once again, and returned to alcohol in excess, if not in addiction.

In July 2008 he got very drunk at his daughter Leah's wedding, and then he was seen in public, later in the month, drinking with a young (19-year-old) Kazakh-Russian woman. In October 2008, he moved out of his home in Ireland, amid rumors of an impending divorce. His autobiography, *Ronnie,* published in 2007, continues to sell reasonably well. His RonnieWood.com blog hasn't had a post by him in over a year.

In January 2009 Ronnie moved to Los Angeles after recording an album there with his old Faces group. He sang at the Rock and Roll Hall of Fame in April and is working on a new solo album, *I Feel Like Playing,* to be out in late 2010.

Charlie Watts has been quite out of the news, the way he seems to like it. There has been no reported recurrence of his throat cancer since the treatment in 2004, and he lives with his wife in their home in England. She is still an active sculptor; he still works with his jazz band and enjoys his various Civil War memorabilia. In both April and May 2009, he made appearances on stage with various artists in British clubs.

Keith Richards owns homes in England (Redlands in Sussex); Weston, Connecticut; and Turks and Caicos. He and his family travel among the houses, although his school-age children are enrolled in a Connecticut school. Though he has "cleaned up his act," he still drinks and prefers Ronnie Wood as his favorite drinking buddy, which doesn't help Wood's problems. Keith seems to have a constitution of iron, considering what and how much he has consumed of various substances. In 2007 he appeared in a brief cameo appearance in *Pirates of the Caribbean: At World's End,* as the father of Jack Sparrow, Johnny Depp's character. Since Depp said he based some of his own mannerisms for the part of Captain Jack Sparrow on Keith Richards, it was only fitting that Keith would appear in the film. He received a cameo award for his role.

Keith was very cooperative with Kris Needs, who authored an excellent biography of Keith in 2004, but in 2007 Keith agreed to do an autobiography, due out in 2010. It would be sensible to assume that he has been working on that book. He made an on-stage appearance at the Musician's Hall of Fame in Nashville in October 2008, for the induction of the Crickets, and he played some of their songs with them. In September 2008 Keith had the lead duets on George Jones's new album, *Burn Your Playhouse Down: The Unreleased Duets.* These were originally recorded in 1994. Keith's official Web site has posted no new news since December 2007.

Mick Jagger has been active in promoting a number of philanthropic causes such as supporting the refugees of Darfur. He did a recording for the United Nations International Day of Peace (September 21, 2009) with Joss Stone. In late 2007 a compilation album, *The Very Best of Mick Jagger,* was released. Despite having four grandchildren, Mick is still in amazing shape and works out on a daily basis, running, lifting, and stretching. He was once compared to the world-renowned dancer Mikhail Baryshnikov in his ability to dance, and the comparison was made by Baryshnikov himself! That was many years ago, but Mick's continued flexibility and powerful dancing continue to amaze. In a June 2009 article Jagger's "secrets" for being in shape were revealed as his great workouts, his moderate drinking, and his healthy diet.[2] Mick continues to "follow the money," accepting sponsorships from almost any corporation willing to pay large sums for promotional use of Stones music or personal appearances. Mick's "politics" seem to be similarly ambiguous.

There have been rumors of a new tour for 2010 but no hints of any recording being done by the Stones, so the rumors of a tour remain just that. It is hard to imagine that the Stones are really finished as a touring or recording group; their style would be to go out with a bang, but maybe the Bigger Bang Tour was intended to be just that. No matter what their decision, their place in history as the greatest rock and roll band is firmly entrenched. There may never be another band to challenge the greatness and longevity of the Rolling Stones.

NOTES

1. Robert Greenfield (2006), *Exile on Main Street: A Season in Hell with the Rolling Stones,* Cambridge, MA: Da Capo Press, p. 239.
2. Edith Grove (2009), "The Mick Jagger Diet," http://www.iorr.org/talk/read.php?1,1082539,1083012, retrieved August 30, 2009.

Appendix: U.S. Albums, 1964–2009 (Stones as Band and Individual Stones)

Album Title	Release Date	Type
The Rolling Stones	April 1964	Studio
12 × 5	October 1964	Studio
The Rolling Stones, Now	February 1965	Studio
Out of Our Heads	September 1965	Studio
December's Children (and Everybody's)	December 1965	Studio
Big Hits (High Tide and Green Grass)	April 1966	Compilation
Aftermath	April 1966	Studio
Got Live If You Want It!	December 1966	Live
Between the Buttons	January 1967	Studio
Flowers	June 1967	Compilation
Their Satanic Majesties Request	December 1967	Studio
Beggars Banquet	December 1968	Studio
Through the Past, Darkly (Big Hits Vol. 2)	September 1969	Compilation
Let It Bleed	December 1969	Studio
Get Your Ya-Ya's Out: The Rolling Stones in Concert	September 1970	Live

Album Title	Release Date	Type
Sticky Fingers	April 1971	Studio
Hot Rocks 1964–71	December 1971	Compilation
Exile on Main St.	May 1972	Studio
More Hot Rocks (Big Hits & Fazed Cookies)	December 1972	Compilation
Goats Head Soup	August 1973	Studio
It's Only Rock 'n Roll	October 1974	Studio
Metamorphosis	June 1975	Compilation
Made in the Shade	June 1975	Compilation
Black and Blue	April 1976	Studio
Love You Live	September 1977	Live
Some Girls	June 1978	Studio
Emotional Rescue	June 1980	Studio
Sucking in the Seventies	March 1981	Compilation
Tattoo You	August 1981	Studio
"Still Life" American Concert 1981	June 1982	Live
Undercover	November 1983	Studio
Rewind (1971–84)	June 1984	Compilation
Dirty Work	March 1986	Studio
Steel Wheels	August 1989	Studio
Singles Collection: The London Years	August 1989	Compilation
Flashpoint	April 1991	Live
Voodoo Lounge	July 1994	Studio
Stripped	November 1995	Live
The Rolling Stones Rock and Roll Circus	October 1996	Live
Bridges to Babylon	September 1997	Studio
No Security	November 1998	Live
Forty Licks	September 2002	Compilation*
Jump Back: The Best of the Rolling Stones	August 2004	Compilation
Live Licks	November 2004	Live
Singles 1968–1971	February 2005	Compilation
A Bigger Bang	September 2005	Studio
Rarities 1971–2003	November 2005	Compilation
Shine a Light	April 2008	Live

*Includes four original studio cuts.

Individual Albums by Rolling Stones Members While Members of the Group

Mick Jagger Albums

Album Title	Release Date	Type
She's the Boss	1985	Studio
Primitive Cool	1987	Studio
Wandering Spirit	1993	Studio
Goddess in the Doorway	2001	Studio
The Very Best of Mick Jagger	2007	Compilation

Keith Richards Albums

Album Title	Release Date	Type
Talk is Cheap	1988	Studio
Live at the Hollywood Palladium, December 15, 1988	1991	Live
Main Offender	1992	Studio

Charlie Watts Albums

Album Title	Release Date	Type
From One Charlie	1991	Studio
Tribute to Charlie Parker with Strings	1992	Studio
Warm & Tender	1993	Studio
Long Ago & Far Away	1996	Studio
Charlie Watts/Jim Keltner Project	2002	Studio
Watts at Scott's	2004	Live

Ron Wood Albums

Album Title	Release Date	Type
I've Got My Own Album to Do	1974	Studio
Now Look	1975	Studio
Mahoney's Last Stand (with Ronnie Lane)	1976	Studio

Gimme Some Neck	1979	Studio
1234	1981	Studio
Live at the Ritz (with Bo Diddley)	1988	Live
Slide on This	1992	Studio
Slide on Live: Plugged in and Standing	1993	Live
Live and Eclectic	2000	Live
Not for Beginners	2001	Live
The Ronnie Wood Anthology: The Essential Crossexion	2006	Compilation

Bill Wyman Albums

Album Title	Release Date	Type
Monkey Grip	1974	Studio
Stone Alone	1977	Studio

Awards

Top Pop Group of 1964	1964	*Melody Maker Magazine*
Best British R&B Band	1967	*New Musical Express*
Best British R&B Band	1968	*New Musical Express*
Rock Album of Year (*Beggars Banquet*)	1968	*Rolling Stone Magazine*
Best Band of 1972	1972	*Billboard Magazine*
Band of the Year	1973	*Creem Magazine*
Best Album (*Exile on Main St.*)	1973	*Creem Magazine*
Best Bass Player (Bill Wyman)	1973	*Creem Magazine*
Top Audience Draw	1975	*Performance Magazine*
Best Group	1975	*Creem Magazine*
Best R&B Band	1975	*Creem Magazine*
Best Live Band	1975	*Creem Magazine*
Best Reissue Album	1975	*Creem Magazine*
Most Valuable Player (Ron Wood)	1975	*Creem Magazine*
Artists of the Year	1978	*Rolling Stone Magazine*
Album of the Year (*Some Girls*)	1978	*Rolling Stone Magazine*

Album of the Year (*Some Girls*)	1978	*New Musical Express*
Band of the Year	1981	*Rolling Stone Magazine*
Best Male Vocalist (Mick Jagger)	1981	*Rolling Stone Magazine*
Album of the Year (*Tattoo You*)	1981	*Rolling Stone Magazine*
Best Songwriters (Jagger/Richards)	1981	*Rolling Stone Magazine*
Best Instrumentalist (Richards)	1981	*Rolling Stone Magazine*
Best Single ("Start Me Up")	1981	*Rolling Stone Magazine*
Inductees, Rock and Roll Hall of Fame	1989	Rock and Roll Hall
Living Legend Award (Keith Richards)	1989	International Rock Awards
Tour of the Year	1989	International Rock Awards
MVP Drummer (Charlie Watts)	1989	International Rock Awards
Outstanding Contribution to British Music	1991	Ivor Novello Awards
Best Rock Album (*Voodoo Lounge*)	1995	Grammy Awards

Further Reading

Andersen, Christopher (1993). *Jagger, Unauthorized.* New York: Delacorte Press.

    Excellent early years, from birth through schools and pregroup formation for Jagger, Jones, Richards.

Appleford, Steve (2000). *The Rolling Stones Rip This Joint: The Stories behind Every Song.* New York: Thunder's Mouth Press.

    Interesting concept. Not exactly a book that one just reads, but the information will be useful and may square with various theories on what some songs mean, as noted in other books.

Booth, Stanley (1985). *The True Adventures of the Rolling Stones.* New York: Vintage Books.

    Booth traveled with the Stones on tours in the late 1960s and provides an insider's look at the band and their various friends and fellow travelers.

Clayson, Alan (2003). *Brian Jones.* London: Sanctuary.

    Difficult to read and get much pointed information. Lots of jargon, meanderings on the scene at the time, and a bit of useful info.

Davis, Stephen (2001). *Old Gods Almost Dead: The 40-Year Odyssey of the Rolling Stones.* New York: Broadway Books.

    Good, historical, and detailed (572 pages) tracing of the Stones.

Faithfull, Marianne, with David Dalton (1994). *Faithfull: An Autobiography.* New York: Cooper Square Press.

    A candid look at Faithfull's life with two-thirds of the book addressing her times with Jagger and the Rolling Stones.

Greenfield, Robert (2006). *Exile on Main Street: A Season in Hell with the Rolling Stones.* Cambridge, MA: Da Capo Press.

A personal description of the Stones during the time, mostly in France, when *Exile on Main Street* was being recorded and the debauchery was at its peak. Written in the literary conceit of a play. Good bibliography but too detailed to offer much that is new and useful conceptually.

Jagger, Mick, Keith Richards, Charlie Watts, and Ronnie Wood (2003). *According to the Rolling Stones.* Edited by Dora Lowenstein and Philip Dodd. London: Weidenfeld and Nicolson.

Twelve chapters that trace chronologically the Stones' history, almost exclusively through commentary from the four principals. Each chapter has an essay by someone involved with the band during that period. These include Ahmet Ertegun, Marshall Chess, and Sheryl Crow. The book has some useful insights and comments. A favorite is from the recollection of Ertegun, involving taking Baryshnikov to see the Stones in concert and later meeting them. His comment to Mick was, "There are only two people who could dance the way you danced tonight. That's you and me."

Needs, Kris (2004). *Keith Richards: Before They Make Me Run.* London: Plexus.

Detailed work by a music writer, DJ, and musician who has known Keith a bit but not enough to be in the inner sanctum. Useful, particularly for the 1990s and early 2000s.

Norman, Philip (1984). *Symphony for the Devil.* New York: Linden Press/ Simon and Schuster.

Ostensibly a tour book (written by an author who toured with the band in 1981–1982), it provides good history, repeats some stories (both factual and apocryphal), and has some useful insight.

Palmer, Robert (1983). *The Rolling Stones.* Garden City, NY: Doubleday.

A coffee-table book and a history from 1963 to 1981 by a well-respected writer from *Rolling Stone* and the *New York Times.* Lots of pictures, not a lot of new information, but a very fast read of the total 264 pages, with some critical insight.

Sanchez, Tony (1979). *Up and Down with the Rolling Stones.* New York: William Morrow.

Personal reflections, anecdotes, and insider dope by a companion, friend, and sometime procurer of drugs during the 1960s and 1970s. Provides more details of some interesting events and sometimes too much detail on some uninteresting nonevents.

Time (1967). "The Baddies." April 28, p. 54.

Short piece on the European tour of 1967.

Wells, Simon (2006). *The Rolling Stones: 365 Days.* New York: Abrams.

A total 744 pages of photos, comments by journalist Wells, and quotes from band members. It begins with a photo of young Basil, "Joe" Jagger, and through to today, moving chronologically.

Wood, Ronnie (2007). *Ronnie: The Autobiography.* New York: St. Martin's Griffin.

A real tell-all with less useful precise data but many good anecdotes and much inside information. Mostly chronological, but not always. The book gives different perspectives on events from Andersen's *Jagger.*

Wyman, Bill, with Ray Coleman (1990). *Stone Alone: The Story of a Rock 'n Roll Band.* New York: Viking.

Wyman (born William Perks) kept *everything* in various scrapbooks and trunks from the beginning of the Stones. These include reviews, handbills, photos, and comments, and his comprehensive pack rat nature makes this book tremendously detailed. It runs nearly 600 pages and includes comments on every Stones event and details on the early years of each of the members.

Wyman, Bill, with Richard Havers (2002). *Rolling with the Stones.* London: DK.

A very big book replicating many of the events of *Stone Alone,* but not as detailed. There are lots of copies of programs, handbills, and photos throughout, making this an interesting book in the coffee-table genre. Goes all the way through Wyman's years in the band.

DVDs and Videos

Lindsey-Hogg, Michael (Director) (1994). *The Rolling Stones Rock and Roll Circus.*

Filmed in December 1968.

Maysles, Albert, and David Maysles (Directors) (1970). *Gimme Shelter.*

The 1969 Altamont concert.

Michaels, Lorne (Director) (1988). *25 × 5: The Continuing Adventures of the Rolling Stones.*

An historical view of the Stones.

Scorsese, Martin (Director) (2008). *Shine a Light.*

Filmed over two nights at the Beacon Theatre in New York City and part of the Biggest Bang Tour.

Web Sites

"Artist: The Rolling Stones, Tour: Bridges to Babylon" (n.d.). http://www.setlist.fm/search?query=artist:%22The+Rolling+Stones%22+tour:%22Bridges+to+Babylon+Tour%22, retrieved May 5, 2009.

"The Bridges to Babylon Tour" (1997). It's Only Rock and Roll. http://www.iorr.org/iorr30/chicago.htm, retrieved May 5, 2009.

"Bridges to Babylon Tour" (n.d.). http://www.absoluteastronomy.com/topics/Bridges_to_Babylon_Tour, retrieved May 5, 2009.

"The Double Door Club Gig" (1997). It's Only Rock and Roll. http://iorr.org/iorr30/door.htm, retrieved May 5, 2009.

Grove, Edith (2009). "The Mick Jagger Diet." http://www.iorr.org/talk/read.php?1,1082539,1083012, retrieved August 30, 2009.

Holland, Doug (1997). "The Horseshoe Tavern Club Gig." It's Only Rock and Roll. http://www.iorr.org/iorr30/horse.htm, retrieved May 5, 2009.

Index

About the Author

MURRY NELSON is professor emeritus of education and American studies at Penn State University and a former Fulbright Scholar in Iceland, Norway, and Hungary. He is also a former public school teacher. He is the author or editor of more than a dozen books and nearly 200 articles. Nelson has been married for nearly 40 years and has two children and a granddaughter.